Filmguide to

2001: A Space Odyssey

D0901864

INDIANA UNIVERSITY PRESS FILMGUIDE SERIES
Harry Geduld and Ronald Gottesman,
General Editors

Filmguide to

2001:
A Space Odyssey

CAROLYN GEDULD

INDIANA UNIVERSITY PRESS
Bloomington London

Published in Canada by Fitzhenry & Whiteside Limited, Don Mills, Ontario
Library of Congress catalog card number: 72–88635
ISBN: 0–253–39305–I cl.   0–253–39306–X pa.
Manufactured in the United States of America

To my parents

Thanks are due to Royal Brown, Ron Gottesman,
William Johnson, Scott Sanders,
and, as always, Harry.

contents

Filmguide to

2001: A Space Odyssey

credits

2001: A SPACE ODYSSEY

Metro-Goldwyn-Mayer, Films, Inc., 1968. Super Panavision, Technicolor and Metrocolor.

Director and Producer	Stanley Kubrick
Screenplay	Stanley Kubrick and Arthur C. Clarke
Production Company	Metro-Goldwyn-Mayer
Special Effects Director	Stanley Kubrick
Special Effects Supervisors	Wally Veevers, Douglas Trumbull, Con Pederson, Tom Howard
Special Effects Photographic Unit	Colin J. Cantwell, Bruce Logan, Bryan Loftus, David Osborne, Frederick Martin, John J. Malick
Production Designers	Tony Masters, Harry Lange, Ernest Archer
Editor	Ray Lovejoy
Wardrobe	Hardy Amies
Director of Photography	Geoffrey Unsworth B.S.C.
Additional Photography	John Alcott
First Assistant Director	Derek Cracknell
Art Director	John Hoesli
Sound Editor	Winston Ryder
Scientific Consultant	Frederick I. Ordway III

Music   Aram Khatchaturian,
                                György Ligeti, Johann
                                Strauss, Richard Strauss
Time: 141 minutes (version in general release)
Filming began on December 29, 1965 in M.G.M.'s Shepperton
   and Boreham Wood Studios in England. First public showing in New York on April 3, 1968.

CAST

Dave Bowman	Keir Dullea
Frank Poole	Gary Lockwood
Dr. Heywood Floyd	William Sylvester
Moon-Watcher	Daniel Richter
Smyslov	
(*the Russian scientist*)	Leonard Rossiter
Elena	Margaret Tyzack
Halvorsen	Robert Beatty
Michaels	Sean Sullivan
HAL's voice	Douglas Rain
Mission Control	Frank Miller
Stewardess	Penny Brahms
Poole's Father	Alan Gifford

outline:

2001: A Space Odyssey

A gigantic pockfaced moon, glorified by Richard Strauss' *Also Sprach Zarathustra,* drifts down the cavernous Cinerama screen. Sunrise is seen on the Earth-crescent hanging above in the sky. So begins the cinematic purple-prose of *2001: A Space Odyssey,* a film in four episodes:

(1) "The Dawn of Man." This title, appearing after the view of sunrise beyond the moon and after the credits, brings us directly to Earth. In silence, we continue with shots taking us from sunrise to sunset on a forbidding primordial half-desert, where a tribe of apes live a kind of minimal existence among a herd of gentle tapirs. One ape (Daniel Richter), called Moon-Watcher in the script, singles himself out as the leader when the mock ferocity of his screams discourages a rival tribe from using the territorial waterhole.

After an ominous night, the awakening apes find that an unnatural object has appeared in their den. It is an outsized black rectangular monolith, made more mysterious by György Ligeti's unearthly requiem slowly swelling in the background. After Moon-Watcher cautiously fingers the monolith, the whole tribe, spellbound, gathers around to caress it as the sun rises "magically" over its roof.

Some time after, we find Moon-Watcher foraging as usual near the broken skeleton of some large, horned animal when—an interrupting shot of the monolith suggests—a new idea enters his consciousness. Tentatively, he picks up one of the larger bones and tries to use it as a cudgel. His efforts become more and more vigorous, and while Strauss' triumphant music drowns out all natural sound, associative shots of a falling ta-pir—the ape-man's first kill—are intercut. Later, at the water-hole, the tribe, armed with bones, kills the weaponless leader of the rivals. Moon-Watcher, victorious, tosses his bone high in the air, and as it comes down, it changes—

(2) —into a man-made satellite orbiting in space four million years later. Rotating to the strains of Johann Strauss' *The Blue Danube,* we see the satellite's companions in space: Earth; a wheel-shaped space station; and the space ship Orion, bringing Dr. Heywood Floyd (William Sylvester), the chairman of the U.S. National Council of Astronauts, from Earth. The docking of Orion and the station completed, Dr. Floyd is cleared by "voice print identification" and waits in the passenger lounge for a connecting flight to the moon. There, he phones his daughter "Squirt" (Vivian Kubrick, the director's daughter) and chats briefly with a party of Rus-sian scientists, who unsuccessfully press for an explanation of the mystery at the American moon-base in the crater Clavius.

The Blue Danube accompanies the spherical space vehicle Aries from the space station to the moon, where Dr. Floyd attends a briefing at Clavius to discuss the top secret object discovered near the base. As Ligeti's *Lux Aeterna* is heard, Dr. Floyd and his colleagues—Halvorsen (Robert Beatty) and Micheals (Sean Sullivan)—travel to the site in a moon bus and talk fleetingly about the strange "rock," recently ex-cavated, that seems to have been "deliberately buried" four million years before. At the excavation, we find another mono-lith and again hear Ligeti's requiem. Immediately after Dr. Floyd circles and warily touches it, the monolith emits a shrill noise, causing the whole party to fall back, stunned.

(3) "Jupiter Mission: 18 months later." The adagio from Khatchaturian's *Gayne Ballet Suite* introduces the spaceship Discovery and her crew of six: three hibernating scientists,

two astronauts—Mission Commander Dave Bowman (Keir Dullea) and his deputy Frank Poole (Gary Lockwood), and a talking computer addressed as HAL (Douglas Rain as HAL's voice). Deep in space, the two on-duty astronauts cope with boredom by jogging, sketching, playing chess with HAL, and monitoring a prerecorded interview with the BBC. From the interview, we learn details about the hibernators, HAL's responsibilities (overseeing the entire operation of the mission) and his "personality," and the ship's destination—Jupiter. A sinister note enters the uneventful ship routine when HAL, ostensibly preparing a psychology report on the crew, points out some incongruities about the nature of the mission. Suddenly, he interrupts the conversation with news of the imminent failure of the AE-35 unit—a component of Discovery's communications network located on the antenna outside of the ship. Bowman uses a spherical "pod"—a vehicle designed for extravehicular activity—to replace the unit which, it is discovered, appears to be in perfect condition. This possible error in judgement raises the question of HAL's reliability. The two astronauts step into a soundproofed pod to discuss the contingency of disconnecting the computer, without realizing that HAL can still see them and is able to read their lips. Meanwhile, they plan to return the supposedly defective unit to the antenna as a cross-check on HAL's accuracy.

An intermission follows, and then we return to the film to find Poole leaving Discovery in the pod and subsequently space-walking to the antenna. At this point, a rapid series of shots reveals that HAL has taken control of the pod and used its mechanical claws to sever Poole's air hose. Bowman, helmetless in a second pod, tries without success to rescue his colleague, only to find that HAL refuses to let him back through the pod-bay door. While the computer "murders" the three hibernating scientists, Bowman enters the emergency air-lock and uses his pod's explosive bolts to blast himself through the vacuum to safety. Back inside the ship, he enters HAL's weightless "logic memory center" and painstakingly disconnects the still-conscious computer. Immediately after, a prerecorded briefing is spontaneously projected on a nearby screen: Dr. Floyd reveals the true purpose of the mission, known only to HAL—to follow an alien radio signal sent to Jupiter by the monolith found on the moon.

(4) "Jupiter and Beyond the Infinite." Ligeti's music, heard throughout much of the last episode, reveals a third monolith, seen floating in the Jovian system, brightened by the Jupiter sunrise. As Bowman rushes toward it in his pod, he "falls" into what scriptwriter Arthur C. Clarke calls the Star Gate, a time-warp represented by "psychedelic" color effects which takes Bowman on an alarming journey to an uncanny room resembling an elegant Eighteenth-century–style bed chamber. There Bowman, already mysteriously aged, is transformed again into an even older man who accidentally breaks his wine glass while dining. The accident signals his third transformation into an ancient bedridden version of himself. As the dying Bowman reaches up and tries to touch it, a fourth monolith appears, enveloping his bed in a strange fog. Out of this comes a huge foetal infant-*in-utero,* the Star Child, who is last seen floating between Earth and the moon as *Also Sprach Zarathustra* welcomes him in the background.

the director:

Previous Odysseys

Stanley Kubrick was born in the Bronx, New York, on July 26, 1928. At thirteen, he owned his first camera, a Graflex given to him by his father, a doctor and amateur photographer. At Taft High School, Kubrick became class photographer, and after graduation, he joined *Look* magazine as staff photographer in April 1945. His informal training as a filmmaker began with readings from the theoretical works of Eisenstein and Pudovkin and heavy attendance at the film programs at the Museum of Modern Art, where he was especially impressed with the works of Ophuls and Welles. In 1950, his film career was launched with a short documentary about a boxer, *Day of Flight,* distributed by R.K.O. In his first four films, he acted as cameraman as well as producer-director, becoming one of the rare directors with membership in the cinematographer's union.

Before *2001,* Kubrick made five films that count, including *Killer's Kiss* (1955), *The Killing* (1956), *Paths of Glory* (1957), *Lolita* (1961), and *Dr. Strangelove* (1963). Those that don't count, taking his own word for it, are his first shoestring efforts of the very early 1950s—*Day of Flight,* a second short called *Flying Padre,* and an unavailable 68-minute feature called *Fear and Desire*—and his Hollywood hackwork on *Spartacus,* a film Kubrick made to finance *Lolita.* He disowns *Spartacus,* claiming to have been just another employee of Kirk Douglas and screenwriter Dalton Trumbo, the *real* auteurs of the project.

Those that do count are the films he was more or less able

to control as director-supreme, supervising every financial and artistic aspect of the filmmaking process from script to publicity with a tough perfectionism generally associated with the Military. For Kubrick, creativity is bound up with beating the system at its own game, a theme that runs concurrently through his life as well as through his films—*2001* in particular. He speaks with relish about the feats he has pulled off under the very noses of the Legion of Decency types in the film industry: embarrassing the French government (*Paths of Glory*), filming the novel that couldn't be filmed (*Lolita*), being flip about nuclear extinction (*Dr. Strangelove*), creating a computer more human than its human creators (*2001*), envisioning man as a savage conditioned to violence (*Clockwork Orange*). The maverick quality of Kubrick's personality and work has been discussed, for example, in Joseph Gelmis' homage to the independent filmmaker, *The Film Director As Superstar,* which places Kubrick in the chapter called "Free Agents Within the System." All of his films since *Paths of Glory* have been money-makers, giving Kubrick the clout necessary to make his kind of film, which might be described as increasingly conceptual, formalistic, provocative—a cinema of rigidly controlled excess.

In a muted way, Kubrick's first two films (that count) anticipate both the control and the excess of *2001* and *A Clockwork Orange. Killer's Kiss* and *The Killing* were made during the final flowering of the *cinéma noir* movement, which was running to seed by the mid-1950s. Although the two films have elements that can now be recognized as uniquely Kubrick's, they are best remembered as classic examples of the *cinéma noir* which featured the blighted environment of dark, rainswept city streets haunted by the corruption and crime of its population of small-time crooks, alcoholic journalists, private eyes, night club personnel; realistic, and often real, locales as sets; expressionistic lighting: a warped chronology always referring to the past; and an overbearing mood of fatalism, hopelessness, paranoia, and confinement.

Killer's Kiss, a 67-minute feature produced, directed, photographed, edited, and scripted by the fledgling Kubrick of 27, has the distinction of being the sleaziest and most unforgivably muddled of his films. The thriller is narrated in a mess of flashbacks and flashbacks within flashbacks by a washed-up boxer who, in an attempt to rescue a woman from a dance hall manager, becomes involved in a chase that leads, vertically, across the rooftops and the deserted streets of New York to a mannequin factory, where the boxer and the manager fight it out with an axe and a window pole among the suggestively broken bodies of dummies. In the long run, however, the chase scenes are somewhat less impressive than the scenes of confinement in the boxer's box-like room, where the heroine can be seen through the window in her room in another part of the building. The boxer watches her, first wistfully, then suspiciously and with a growing sense of menacing fatalism, much as Humbert would watch his nymphet in *Lolita* seven years later and as HAL would watch the astronauts in *2001*. Like Lolita, the archetypal good-bad girl-child, the heroine of *Killer's Kiss* is typical of the good-bad women of the *cinéma noir* period, richly described by Martha Wolfenstein and Nathan Leites in *Movies: A Psychological Study* (1950) as the basically good women who only appears to be bad because of her association with a bad man. Kubrick's heroine actually does betray the boxer-hero out of fear, but she is redeemed at the last minute by agreeing to leave New York with the waiting hero.

The boxer in *Killer's Kiss* follows in the tradition of early *cinéma noir* Bogart-like heroes of the 1940's—hard-boiled softies who adopt a cynical tough-minded style to cover up for their secret (and ultimately winning) emotionalism. Variations on this type appear again in Kubrick's films in the character of

Colonel Dax in *Paths of Glory* and Humbert in *Lolita,* but disappear thereafter in favor of the kind of hero Kubrick would develop to perfection in *The Killing.* This is the later *cinema noir* hero of the 1950s, whom Paul Shrader described as "post–hardboiled" in "Notes on Film Noir" (*Film Comment,* Spring 1972). For these heroes, men like Richard Widmark, James Cagney, and Lee Marvin, romantic emotionalism is replaced by psychosis, protective cynicism by sadism, tough-mindedness by the mania of a total martinet. In Kubrick's films, they would become cold-blooded, inhuman, "robotized", and at worst, insane or brutal to the core.

The Killing, Kubrick's first film to earn a critical reputation, puts Sterling Hayden in the "robotized" role of the boss of a gang brought together to pull off a race track robbery. Unlike the unstructured excesses of *Killer's Kiss, The Killing* represents Kubrick's first "clockwork" film, a rigid attempt to control time in the way that *2001* would attempt to control space. The robbery is planned by Hayden with a minute-by-minute maniacal efficiency. ("He knew exactly how long it would take him to drive to the track, park his car, and walk to the grandstand.") The ferocity of Hayden's control is emphasized both by the impersonal semi-documentary narration which alludes to the third-person workings of Hayden's mind and by the back-tracking of the last part of the film, which shows how each member of the gang in turn sticks or fails to stick to the timetable during the actual robbery. Hayden's overly programmed sense of time, however, is always a shade out of step with the unpredictabilities of "real" time. Towards the end, "real" time begins to fight back with small accidents of fate that violate Hayden's timetable—a traffic jam, a broken suitcase, a punctured tire, an unleashed dog. In the final scene, the racetrack money falls out of Hayden's suitcase and is scattered all over an airfield in full view of the waiting police. Unable to flee, Hayden is paralyzed, mentally disconnected like HAL when his program fails.

In keeping with the hardening of the *cinéma noir* tradition, the good-bad woman of *Killer's Kiss* is frozen into the out and out bitch of *The Killing*. Marie Windsor, playing the unfaithful wife of gang member Elisha Cook, is the unpredictable factor who dooms everyone in the film, except Hayden, by bringing on a shoot-out in the boss's absence. Fittingly, the gang members are shown frozen in the grotesque postures of violent death after the shoot-out—a visual counterpart of the paralysis of Hayden at the airfield. Typically for a Kubrick film, they individually represent an externalization of the borderline madness Hayden conceals with his own mania: marksman Tim Carey spewing eccentricities through a locked jaw; little Elisha Cook dreading impotency; muscle man Kola Kwariani smashing English with his thick accent as he will later smash men.

The Killing is a film whose every nuance suggests an inescapable, predetermined fate that overrides individual man's small scale plans and programs and places him in the unheroic position of the manipulated rather than the manipulator. While *2001* would eventually pick up and amplify this theme, it originates as a basic attitude expressed by most *cinéma noir* films. What Kubrick would do after *The Killing* is to take the *cinéma noir* hero and the *cinéma noir* psychology and project them as they are, only more and more so, into the non–*cinéma noir* genres of the later 1950s, 1960s, and 1970s. HAL is simply the remotest possibility of what Sterling Hayden in *The Killing* could become, via Peter Seller's wacky inhumanity in *Lolita* and *Dr. Strangelove*.

The transitional film in this scheme is *Paths of Glory,* which pits Kirk Douglas as Colonel Dax, the hard-boiled softy, against George Macready as General Mireau, the "robotized" zealot, in a war situation where the arbitrariness of fate is heightened beyond all human preplanning. The war in this case is World War I, weighted with a meaninglessness all its own in distinction to the clear-cut issues and choices of World War II. In the midst of a ponderous sense of helplessness and predestined doom, Kubrick poses the question of what kind of creature man is—an ineffectual quasi humanist like Dax or a cold-blooded but powerful killer like Mireau. The difference between the two men appears in this film as a factor of class. Their conflict takes place behind the French lines (the Germans are never seen), where Dax, a lawyer in civilian life, is quartered with the common soldiers in the trenches and Mireau, with the higher command in an elegant chateau—an anticipation in its eighteenth-century décor of the alien "hotel" room in *2001*.

Essentially, Dax is a technician, a predecessor of Dave Bowman with a weakness for humanism. He wishes simply to get the job done, although he would like a fair shake for the men in his command. He never rebels against the war or military life, but he insists that they be played according to the "rules." Mireau, on the other hand, is the technician obsessed by glory, the glory of promotion within the French army, and like *2001*'s HAL, he will break all the rules if his particular path to glory is blocked. At the opening of the film, he is informed that he will be in line for another star if Dax's battle-weary regiment can take the ant hill, an impregnable German stronghold. At first Mireau resists. The assault is clearly impossible to accomplish. But by a process of gradual distancing from the realities of potential human suffering, a kind of computerization of the mind, the general convinces himself that the assault might succeed—and that in any case, he'd better make the attempt. When asked to estimate the casualties, his response is a bonechilling abstraction: "5 percent, killed by our own barrage; 10 percent more going through no man's land; and 20 percent more again going through the wire. That leaves 65 percent. And the worst part of the job over."

The command to attack, however, arrives during a morning of heavy German barrage, and most of Dax's troops cannot leave the trenches, or are killed trying. In a cold fury, Mireau orders the battery commander to fire on his own positions to force the men out of the trenches. When this order is refused, he arranges a court martial under penalty of death for cowardice for a hundred men. After much negotiation, Adolphe Menjou as General Broulard—a more cautious and wily Mireau-type—arranges for three men to stand trial. Dax acts as defense for the accused, but the trial is a farce and the three scapegoats are executed. The eleventh-hour discovery of Mireau's order to fire on his troops does not move General Broulard to leniency toward the three doomed men, but Mireau, now facing court martial himself, commits suicide, effectively "disconnecting" himself when his plan collapses.

The contest between the humanist and the zealot seems pretty much a draw. Mireau is dead, but so are his three innocent victims. Broulard, however, is alive and all the more powerful, while Dax, having refused an offer of an easy path to glory himself, is left three steps behind where he started. At this point, Kubrick ends the film with an additional scene. Dax discovers his troops in a tavern, jeering at a frightened German girl captured by the French tavern owner and forced to perform for them. When the girl sings a simple song, the soldiers soften and listen with tears in their eyes. The possibilities embraced by Mireau and Dax are universal; man is as much one as the other, and in *Paths* tear-streaked man is given the bare edge over the professional zealots in the end.

Lolita is Kubrick's comic study of the same problem, although in comedy Kubrick assumes a much harder line. In the adaptation of Nabokov's novel about a middle-aged man's infatuation for a "nymphet" (the thirteen-year-old Lolita), all the forces of paranoia, hopelessness, and confinement erupt in a setting of outward normalcy—the resort town of Ramsdale, New Hampshire. For the first time in a Kubrick film, these forces exist without the external justification of a war or a violent city situation, leaving James Mason as Humbert—the hero who experiences them—at insurmountable odds with surrounding reality. Dax could not leave the trenches because of enemy barrage; Humbert, with the world open before him (no one in Ramsdale really cares about his "crime of passion") imprisons himself in bathrooms, cars, motel rooms, folding cots, and very nearly in a hospital strait jacket.

Unlike Kubrick's other heroes, Humbert can cope neither with mechanical objects, like cots and guns, nor with everyday social occasions, like the town dance or the twitter of Ramsdale's "young marrieds," nor with the workings of his own body: he gets the flu and dies of a heart condition at the end of the film. For Kubrick, there is something both pathetic and funny about a man who is at a loss as a technician, especially when circumstances demand a good amount of engineering and control. In Ramsdale, Humbert finds himself in a time-trap, as Hayden did in *The Killing.* His obsession for Lolita is threatened both by the girl's natural aging (she won't be a "nymphet" for long) and by the boarding school in which she might be prematurely cloistered. In the short space of a summer, he must marry her mother (Shelley Winters), ease the girl out of attachments to boyfriends of her own age, become a widower, and seduce Lolita. It all happens, not as planned but through a series of accidents: Humbert is manipulated by some sort of programmed fate, and the film is comic as long as fate works for him in spite of his worst efforts.

Peter Sellers as Quilty, Lolita's other grown-up seducer, is a madcap continuation of the Hayden- and Mireau-types, a "robotized" supertechnician who has control over everything Humbert bungles. Kubrick claims it was censorship restrictions that forced him to shift the focus of the film away from Lolita's eroticism and toward the relationship of the two men who want her. Characteristically, Humbert and Quilty again set the lesser technician with feeling and the greater, manic technician in opposition. This time, the differences between the two emerge as a factor of culture. Humbert is the European intellectual; Quilty, the pop-cultured American pornographer (who nevertheless, like Mireau, lives in a castle while Humbert is confined to the "trenches" of middle-brow America). But while the differences between Dax and Mireau are easily distinguished in *Paths of Glory,* the opposing traits of the two men in *Lolita* tend to overlap. Humbert must pretend to have assimilated vulgar American attitudes from time to time and Quilty, in the disguise of Dr. Zempf, reverts to the role of European intellectual. As Pauline Kael has pointed out, Quilty is less an individual than a projection of Humbert's paranoia: he chases Humbert and Lolita across the country until Humbert is forced to "disconnect" him in a zany shoot-out that opens the film. Even though both Quilty and Humbert die, there is never a doubt about Quilty's superiority. He kidnaps Lolita, charms Ramsdale, and outwits Humbert at every turn. From *Lolita* on, it is the Quilties who inherit the earth, even if in their insanity they manage to destroy it at the same time.

After Ramsdale, Kubrick moved his films out of small time settings to the larger scenarios of world-wide disaster in *Dr. Strangelove, or How I Learned to Stop Worrying and Love the Bomb* (1963) and interstellar confrontation in *2001,* but retaining the vestiges of his earlier *cinéma noir* interests. *Dr. Strangelove* is the projection of the paranoia not of a man, but of an entire decade—the Fifties, with its half-crazed fear of the Bomb.

With the help of Terry Southern and Peter George, Kubrick prepared the film as a straight adaptation of Peter George's novel, *Red Alert,* a serious study of human weakness in a nuclear deterence system (in contrast to machine weakness in *2001*'s computerized space program). The novel argues that the President alone could not have access to the big button, and that someone with access further down the line might be a secret psychotic. Borrowing *Lolita's* suggestion of the off-beat sexuality that motivates even the "sane" man, Kubrick transformed *Red Alert* into a black comedy in which the fate of the world lies in the hands of a group whose sexual or sexually-determined anxieties have gone wildly out of control.

Once again, Kubrick divides the group into the "robots" and the fumbling humanists, who by now are ineffectual to the point of invisibility. Sterling Hayden reappears in a Kubrick film as General Jack D. Ripper, who activates an irreversible B-52 nuclear attack on Russia when he feels his "precious bodily fluids" threatened by a "Communist conspiracy" to poison American drinking water. Peter Sellers (playing three roles) as Captain Lionel Mandrake, another restrained European, is too caught up in his correct British upper-crustiness to stop Ripper, although they are locked in the same room. A few miles away in the Pentagon's spacious War Room, recalling Mireau's chateau and Quilty's castle, the faint-hearted President Muffley (Peter Sellers) and his advisors meet to cope with the crisis. George C. Scott as General "Buck" Turgidson, first heard talking to his mistress through a bathroom door, views the human consequences of the attack as a mathematical abstraction similar to Mireau's in *Paths of Glory:* "I'm not saying we wouldn't get our hair mussed. I am saying only ten to twenty million people killed, tops, depending on the breaks."

But he doesn't figure on the Doomsday Machine, designed to trigger a global nuclear holocaust if either America or Russia precipitates an attack. The device is the invention of the ex-Nazi, Dr. Strangelove (Peter Sellers), who emerges from the shadows of the War Boom like a bizarre fiend, recalling Fritz Lang's satanic Rotwang in the classic German expressionist film, *Metropolis.* Indeed, Strangelove proves to be a half-robot with a mechanical hand and a motorized wheel chair. In him, Kubrick locks machine and man in a wierd, sexualized (as his name suggests) union. The mechanical parts of Strangelove are autonomous, the hand threatening to choke him or snap into an unauthorized *Sieg Heil* while his face is stamped with a fixed grin, like HAL's neutral voice-print, concealing deeper evil. Strangelove—the projection of modern man's insanity—completes the fusion of technology, sex, and death with his vision of an underground shelter stocked with ravishing women. Making the point even more explicit, Slim Pickens as Major "King" Kong, piloting the attacking B-52, straddles the bomb as if it were a gigantic phallus and drops with it toward the ultimate orgasm of nuclear explosion. At the moment of detonation, in the War Room, Strangelove stands and shouts, "Mein Fuehrer, I can walk!" Not a Star Child, but a newly energized machine-man is born as the planet comes down around his ears.

In Kubrick's "comedies," the more machine-like intelligences always get the better of mere men. Following *2001,* Kubrick used comedy to experiment with the idea of a whole society of Dr. Strangeloves in *A Clockwork Orange,* based on Anthony Burgess' novel. Set in the near future, it populates England with a breed who have so incorporated the worst of machine values that the external presence of tools is no longer quite necessary. In an environment relatively free of technology, the teenage hero, Alex, takes pleasure in "ultraviolence"—the beating, rape, and even killing of whoever happens to cross his path. The government, which occasionally finds it prudent to control Alex and his gang, uses the "Ludovico Treatment," a form of conditioning therapy, to turn their aggression on or off. Alex becomes a "clockwork," a virtual robot to be played with by a higher authority, programmed as is man by the aliens in *2001*.

Like his themes, the production values Kubrick has brought to his films have been remarkably consistent throughout his career. The kind of bravado cinematography that characterizes *2001* was already evident in *Killer's Kiss*, with its lighting from dramatic but natural sources, mobile camera, distorting lenses in moments of stress, a dream sequence in negative tracking rapidly down an empty street (anticipating *2001*'s Star Gate effect), great attention to authentic detailing, continual contrast of confining and open spatial arrangements, frequent shots in depth through tunnels and corridors, and a tendency to break up the screen as often as possible with miniature figures seen through windows, mirrors, television sets. Kubrick used music and sound effects inventively for the first time in *Dr. Strangelove,* most memorably in his ironic choice of "We'll Meet Again" during the nuclear explosion, but his dialogue was unremarkable until Nabokov taught him the ironic resonances of ordinary small talk in *Lolita,* which was later developed into the space jargon of *2001* and "nadsat," the language of *A Clockwork Orange*.

The difference between *2001* and the Kubrick films that preceded it are not so much differences of form or content as differences of budget and freedom of hand. What distinguishes *2001* from the other films is that in it Kubrick had the kind of resources and innovative techniques at his disposal to expand his vision to epic scale.

the production:

a Calendar

1902 In France, George Méliès makes what is perhaps the first
science fiction film, *A Trip to the Moon,* a sixteen minute production.

1926 Hugo Gernsback publishes the first American hard-core
science fiction magazine, *Amazing Stories,* creating a
brand new kind of buff—the Space Opera fan.

1930s First working automatic computers built. In 1930, Dr.
Vannevar Bush completes the first general purpose *analog* computer at the Massachusetts Institute of Technology. In 1939, Dr. George R. Stibitz builds the first *digi-
tal* computer for Bell Telephone Laboratories in New
York. *2001*'s HAL (for *H*euristically programmed *AL*-
gorithmic computer) is an advanced hybrid of these
two original types of computers.

1948 Arthur C. Clarke writes his short story, "The Sentinel."
Superman, film's first Star Child, arrives from the planet
Krypton in a Columbia movie serial based on the comic
strip originally conceived by Jerry Siegel and Joe Schuster in 1938.

1950s High-water mark for science-fiction films. Directors like
George Pal and Byron Haskin in films like *Destination
Moon* (1950) and *The Conquest of Space* (1955) ran-
sack the special effects departments in attempts to create authentic-looking space technology consistent with
the scientific ideas of the day.

1960 B.B.C. televises a science fiction serial with close affinities to *2001*—Nigel Kneale's *Quatermass and the Pit* (remade in a film version by Hammer Film Productions as *Five Million Years to Earth* in 1967). In one episode, while excavating to enlarge the London underground, a five-million-year old alien artifact is discovered. Near it lies the ape ancestors of man whose skulls have been surgically modified to increase intelligence.

Universe, an award-winning 28-minute black-and-white animated documentary is produced by the National Film Board of Canada. It is to become the inspiration for *2001's* panning shots of slowly revolving planets and moving stars in deep space. In 1965, Kubrick tries to hire *Universe's* special effects team of Wally Gentleman, Herbert Taylor, and James Wilson. Wally Gentleman agrees to do a few months' preparatory work on *2001* before a sudden illness forces him to abandon the project.

1964 *Spring.* Kubrick contacts Clarke and asks him to collaborate on a sci-fi film.

April. Clarke leaves his home in Ceylon for his first meeting with Kubrick in New York. Kubrick suggests the unorthodox procedure of writing a novel together before writing a script, a project that was to take two years to complete.

May. Kubrick agrees to use Clarke's "The Sentinel" as the central idea for the novel. The discovery of the alien artifact on the moon is to be the climax of the story. Meanwhile, Kubrick views every available science fiction film.

July 31. Ranger VII sends close-up pictures of the moon back to Earth before crashing on the lunar surface.

August 6. "Female" computer called Athena written into novel.

November. Gathering of ideas of what is to be the "Dawn of Man" episode. This is intended to be a flashback interrupting the main story.

December 25. Clarke finishes the first 50,000 word draft of the novel, which ends at the Star Gate sequence. Kubrick is able to sell the idea for a film based on this draft to M.G.M. and Cinerama. The film's projected budget is $6 million.

1965 *February 21.* M.G.M. press release announcing forthcoming production of a Kubrick film to be called "Journey Beyond the Stars."

March 18. Aleksei A. Leonav, a Russian astronaut, becomes the first man to "walk" in space.

Spring. Clarke revises novel. Kubrick begins to hire staff (35 designers, 20 special effects technicians, a total of 106 people) and cast for the production. "The Sentinel" pyramid is changed to a black tetrahedron, then a transparent cube, finally a black rectangular block—the monolith.

April. Kubrick selects *2001: A Space Odyssey* as the new title for the film.

May. Clarke works on possible endings for the novel.

June 3. Ed White becomes the first American to "walk" in space, bettering Leonav's feat by 20 minutes.

June 14. Mariner IV comes within 6,200 miles of Mars and sends 22 photographs of the planet's surface back to Earth. Kubrick contacts Lloyds of London to price an insurance policy against Martians being discovered before the release of his film.

August. After a brief return to his home in Ceylon, Clarke joins Kubrick at the M.G.M. studios in Boreham Wood near London. There, sets are being built, the most meticulously detailed models ever made for a film are being constructed over a period of months, costumes are being designed and executed with an eye toward fashions 35 years in the future, and the ape makeup and costuming are being developed over the course of a year.

October 3. The final decision about the ending of the film is reached. Bowman will turn into an infant.

October 15. Kubrick decides that Bowman should be the only surviving member of Discovery's crew.

December 29. First day of shooting in Shepperton studio near London which is spacious enough to accommodate oversized sets. Kubrick films the scene in the moon excavation in the Tycho crater. The set is a huge 60 by 120 by 60 foot pit constructed on the second largest stage in Europe. Background details of the lunar terrain and the miniature Earth in the sky are added a year later.

1966 *January.* Production moves to the smaller Boreham Wood studios. Kubrick films scenes on board Orion. Clarke finishes draft of novel, adding HAL's rebellion and alien hotel room to plot.

February 2. Makeup tests for Gary Lockwood and Keir Dullea, who remain in the studio for seven months of filming.

February 3. First soft landing on the moon by an unmanned Russian spacecraft.

February 4. Screening of "demonstration film" for Metro Goldwyn Mayer, consisting of a few completed scenes, including shots of the interiors of the space station and the moon shuttle. Mendelssohn's *Midsummer Night's Dream* and Vaughan Williams' *Antartica Symphony* are used on the sound track.

March–April. Shooting inside Discovery's ferris-wheel–

shaped centrifuge. The Vickers Engineering Group builds a real one for the production at a cost of $750,-000. The wheel is 40 feet in diameter and rotates at 3 miles per hour. A closed circuit television system enables Kubrick to direct the filming from outside the wheel. Inside, two kinds of camera setups are used: either the camera is attached to the set and rotates with it (used when the actors appear to be climbing the centrifuge walls) or the camera is secured to a small dolly which remains with the actors at the bottom of the rotating set (used when Poole jogs). Kubrick plans to put a Chopin waltz on the soundtrack during the astronauts' routine activities.

May. Clarke visits Hollywood to promote the film and placate worried M.G.M. executives.

June. Clarke returns to Boreham Wood. He tries unsuccessfully to convince Kubrick to allow publication of the novel before the release of the film.

June 2. First soft landing on the moon by an unmanned American spacecraft, Surveyor I.

December. Original target date for film's release.

1967 *January–February.* Composer Alex North records his music for *2001* in London, until Kubrick changes his mind about using an original score for the film.

Most of the year is devoted to completing the film's exacting and complex special effects, a job taking more than 18 months and costing $6,500,000 out of a total budget of $10,500,000. 205 shots (about half the film) require process work. Each shot involves an average of 10 major laboratory steps to complete. Counting the high number of retakes, an estimated 16,000 separate shots are taken for the 205 effects. Most of these are "held takes," that is, a portion of a scene is filmed, then the negative is filed away for several months until another element can be filmed and added to the original. (Part of Kubrick's great achievement is that there is no noticeable loss of crispness in the image, despite all the tampering with the negative.) A typical special effects shot might include (1) miniature models of space craft shot in extremely slow motion, (2) front or rear projected film for the moving images in the space craft's windows, (3) a separately photographed astronaut or pod tumbling in space (both suspended by wires during shooting) "matted" in by hand, (4) a field of moving stars in the background shot on the animation stand along with (5) the moon (a series of actual astronomical plates) and/or an appropriate planet (usually a large painting).

Two techniques developed by Kubrick's special effects team are especially significant for the future of the film industry. (1) The front-projection system, seen throughout the "Dawn of Man" episode, is a new way of using a still photograph as a background for a shot. A unique kind of projector throws an image onto a mammoth screen, without being visible on the cast or props in the foreground, making it economically feasible to film large-scale epics in the sound studio without the expense of going "on location." (2) The Slit-Scan machine, designed for the Star Gate sequence, produces a fast-moving tunnel of lights and shapes that seems to extend to infinity. The machine keeps the image in focus from a distance of fifteen feet to an incredible one-half inch from the lens.

1968 *March 13*. Kubrick returns to the United States. While the last special effects shots are still coming in, he edits the film. Several scenes are omitted, including the purchase of a bushbaby for Dr. Floyd's daughter, Squirt; routine activities on the moon; shots of the astronaut's families; shots of the ping-pong table, shower, and piano in Discovery. After a screening for the M.G.M. executives in Culver City, California, Kubrick cuts the prologue and all voice-over narration from the film.

March 29. Screening of the film for *Life* magazine.

March 31, April 1. Washington press previews.

April. The discovery of a man-like jaw bone in southern Ethiopia pushes man's history back to the 4 million year mark.

April 1, 2. New York press previews of the film in Loew's Capital Cinerama Theatre.

April 3. New York premiere in the Capitol Theatre.

April 4. Los Angeles premiere.

April 4, 5. Kubrick cuts 19 minutes from the film's original running time of two hours and forty-one minutes, shortening scenes including "Dawn of Man," Orion, Poole jogging in Discovery, and Poole in the pod.

April 6. Final version released in New York in the Cinerama Theatre on Broadway, 16 months late and at a cost of $4,500,000 over the original budget of $6 million.

Early April. Kubrick edits the *2001* trailer.

July. Publication of Clarke's novel, *2001: A Space Odyssey.* The paperback edition sale exceeds one million copies.

December 21. Apollo VIII carries man into a moon orbit for the first time.

1969 *April.* Kubrick receives an Oscar for special effects; three British Film Academy awards for cinematography, art direction, and soundtrack; and the Italian film industry's David Di Donatello award for the best film from the West.

July 20. Neil Armstrong and Edwin Aldrin walk on the moon.

1970 *April.* Publication of Jerome Agel's *The Making of Kubrick's 2001.*

1971 *November 28.* The first conscious imitation of *2001,* M.G.M.'s made-for-TV film, *Earth II,* televised in New York. Gary Lockwood stars and footage, effects, and plot structure are strikingly similar to *2001.*

1972 *January.* Publication of Arthur C. Clarke's *The Lost Worlds of 2001.*

January 5. Variety puts *2001* in 24th place in its annual compilation of "All-Time Boxoffice Champs." It estimates that the film has grossed more than $21,500,000 in the U.S.-Canada market alone.

February. Publication of Arthur C. Clarke's *Report on Planet Three.*

March 2. Pioneer X launched on course toward Jupiter and beyond.

2001 "What we are trying to create is a realistic myth—and we may have to wait until the year 2001 itself to see how successful we have been." (Arthur C. Clarke, *Report on Planet Three,* p. 246.)

5 ·

analysis:

". . . some extremely odd things about this mission."

In the films he made before *2001,* Kubrick asked what kind of being man is—a soft creature of feeling or a hard creature of abstract intelligence? By *Dr. Strangelove,* he seemed to have the answer: man was essentially a creature of abstract intelligence, although his abstraction, used in the service of his sexual drive, was tantamount to insanity. He *deserved* to be destroyed by his own hand. In *2001,* however, Kubrick renews the whole issue of the essential nature of man in a more exhaustive way. He asks historical questions about the separation of feeling and intelligence. How did one come to dominate the other, and where did the other one "go"? Did an external event, like a visitation from another planet, change the balance in man's divided nature, or even cause the initial division? Probing deeper, he asks if his model of man's nature is universal, a variant of a natural structure that exists across time and across space. Finally, he asks if this universal model expresses itself through myth. At the deepest level, it is the mythology of intelligence that *2001* is all about.

The basic conflict in the film is between ideas that are philosophical and ideas that are unconscious, as Kubrick believes mythology must be. As Clarke has acknowledged in *Report on Planet Three* (1972), "all the mythical elements in the film— intentional or otherwise—help to explain the extraordinarily powerful responses that it has evoked from audiences and re-

29

viewers" (pp. 247–48). Kubrick uses a sophisticated style to force us to "think" mythically, taking as his starting point an adaptation of Clarke's story, "The Sentinel." Internal evidence suggests, however, that for Kubrick, the story is just another cinematic tool. It is used to create a receptive mood for a vision that is basically beyond narrative.

For Clarke, on the other hand, the narrative is a frankly serious study of scientific and metaphysical speculations about the existence of extraterrestrials and their possible involvements on Earth. In *Report on Planet Three,* he informs us that "planets are at least as common as stars—of which there are some 100 billion in our local Milky Way galaxy alone. Moreover, it is believed that life will arise automatically and inevitably where conditions are favorable; so there may be civilizations all around us which achieved space travel before the human race existed" (p. 239). He adds that Earth may already have been visited by extraterrestrials in the past, a thought "which I now more than half believe myself" (p. 239). As Clarke tells it in *The Lost Worlds of 2001,* he had brought "The Sentinel," written in 1948 as an elaboration of this possibility, to the attention of Kubrick early in 1964. The central idea of the story, which ran to little more than ten pages in its first printing in Clarke's *Expedition to Earth* (1954), remained constant through four years of the extensive reworkings that ultimately led to the expanded book version and the film.

In conception, "The Sentinel" is not so much a story as a science fiction situation, described in first person by a rather aloof hero. It takes place in 1996, after the first permanent bases have been established on the moon but before the lunar surface has been fully explored. The hero, a geologist and selenologist, is in charge of a group exploring the great Sea of Crisis, or Mare Crisium, five hundred miles from the main lunar base in Mare Serenitatis. Both the distance from headquarters and the barrenness of the surroundings awaken rebel instincts in the hero, who is tantalized by the unexplored mountains circling the Mare, especially when he notices a strangely symmetrical "metallic glitter" on one of the peaks. Risking ridicule, he decides to investigate with his skeptical assistant, and, after a long and difficult climb, they reach an unnaturally smooth plateau, one hundred feet wide. In the middle sits a "glittering roughly pyramidal structure, twice as high as a man," surrounded by an invisible protective shield. Because all the planets in the solar system have been explored for life and found wanting, the hero concludes that the pyramid, obviously deposited there by intelligent agents, must have come from the stars.

Twenty years later, in the year 2016, the invisible shield has been demolished by atomic force and the pyramid is destroyed without ever having been understood. The hero, who at this point (traditionally for science-fiction) remains the only man aware of the human folly he was unable to stop, ventures his opinion about the pyramid. The aliens, he suggests, were the first "masters of the universe," but suffered the "loneliness of gods" which led them, millions of years ago, to search for other forms of intelligent life. After predicting that intelligence would evolve on Earth, the aliens left a sentinel on the moon in the form of the protected pyramid, which until 2016 had been "patiently signalling the fact that no one had discovered it." Once mankind had established credibility as an intelligent civilization by conquering atomic energy and reaching the moon, the triggering of the solar alarm left by the aliens—who knew the pyramid had been found when the mechanism was smashed and the signalling stopped—would presumably bring them to Earth. Finally, the hero speculates about the attitude of the aliens, who may be friendly, or, more ominously, "insanely jealous of the young."

Clarke was to toy with the idea of the sentinel more than

once in the late 1940s and early 1950s. Indeed, in *Expedition to Earth* alone, two other stories are concerned with sentinels, although in the title story, the device is left by the last man during a future ice age for possible detection by alien visitors, and in "Loophole," the aliens who use a sentinel to detect experiments with rocket propulsion on Earth tell their side of the story. Without looking far beyond this single representative anthology of Clarke's work, traces can be found of almost all the plot material in *2001,* save the final episode. In both "Encounter in the Dawn" and "Second Dawn," for instance, a superior but either limited or dying alien civilization guides a more primitive life form up the evolutionary ladder; in "Breaking Strain," an accident in space leaves only one member of a two member crew alive; in "Superiority" and "Hide-and-Seek," human intelligence is given the edge over runaway computerized technology. Most of Clarke's stories of this period deal, generally, with the instinctual destructiveness of mankind which interferes with the purified intellect of either the aliens or the future civilizations that must, out of mere interest or necessity, protect themselves. The relationship between man and alien in these stories is rather like that of a very young child and either a good parent, who must gently and unobtrusively elicit conscience as well as consciousness in his offspring, or a bad parent who murders the troublesome child who cannot be domesticated.

Yet, for Clarke, the relationship between man and alien often seems less important than establishing the alien-ness of the aliens. In the early prose versions of *2001,* the plot material unused in the film—the Earth background of all the astronauts, the role of the rather innocuous computer called Athena and her even less sinister twin on Earth called Socrates, the completely innocent accidents in space that kill Whitehead and Poole and permanently sever communications with Mission Control—still serve to bring Bowman alone through the Star Gate where he can directly confront extraterrestrial life. In the three published versions of the early attempts to find a suitable ending for Bowman's journey (printed in *The Lost Worlds of 2001*), Clarke borrows heavily from Olaf Stapledon's classic science-fiction novel, *Starmaker* (1937), which describes an organic universe populated with all sorts of improbable intelligences, from wheel-legged metal crabs to civilized suckerfish to parapsychic plant life. It appears to have been Kubrick's decision to turn the camera from the aliens back to mankind, in part because of his dissatisfaction with attempts to film convincing extraterrestrials. (A few stills from these abortive attempts are reproduced in Agel's *The Making of Kubrick's 2001*.)

In the released film, the emphasis is so securely on man that the aliens are suggested only by indirection. Gone is the humanoid named Clindar who handed Moon-Watcher his first tool in *The Lost Worlds of 2001,* while the nature of the lunar monolith—an open secret in Clarke's early version—becomes a mystery even for Bowman, who never sees his alien hosts. Kubrick's decision is further reflected in his change of the film's title. Until April 1965, the work was to be called "Journey Beyond the Stars." The switch to *2001: A Space Odyssey,* however, clearly anchors the film to Earth by giving it an Earth date, suggesting that the journey's end is our home planet, lest we forget Homer's original thought that all "odysseys" are really roundtrips.

Nevertheless, Kubrick was still hovering between a more extensive use of Clarke's story and his own nonnarrative methodology right until the first screening of *2001* for M.G.M. executives, when he decided to cut the ten-minute prologue that was to have opened the film. This prologue, which survives in an abridged printed form in Agel's book, consists of interviews separately filmed by Roger Caras in black-and-white. In it, a number of leading scientists, like A. I. Oparin of Moscow's Academy of Sciences and F. C. Dumant III of the Smithsonian Institute, speculate about the possibilities of man communicating with extraterrestrial beings, and a theologian, Rabbi Norman Lamm of Yeshiva University, reassures us of God's probable approval of the project. At the time Kubrick made this cut, he also ruthlessly slashed every bit of explanatory narration from the film, leaving as his only concessions to Clarke the three titles that introduce the first, third, and fourth episodes. In effect, the early cuts made by Kubrick took much of the science out of the film's science fiction. But the shadowy drift further and further away from Clarke's explicit prose is part of *2001*'s great achievement and great allure. Kubrick relies almost entirely on the deeper resonances evoked by image and structure to express ideas that may not really be so remote from mankind's experience as outer space.

It has already been noted that Kubrick's cinema might be called the cinema of rigidly controlled excess. As it stands, the excessive streak in *2001* is found in its style (images and cutting), while the rigid control is evident in its highly formalistic structure. Kubrick seems to be fascinated by the number four. *2001*, which took four years to complete, is divided into four episodes, covers four million years, has four heroes (ape, scientist, machine, astronaut), concerns four evolutions (man, machine, alien, the universe), uses the music of four composers (the two Strausses, Ligeti, and Khatchaturian), and is dominated by a four-sided rectangle that appears on screen four times. The number four crops up ritualistically throughout the film, something not accounted for by Clarke. It creates an obsessively rhythmic force in the film that refers to the "clockwork" mechanism, common to all of Kubrick's work, holding the "mythological" side of his "mythological documentary" (as he calls *2001*) in check.

Even before the main credits, the film opens with a shot that dramatically sets the tone for the whole work while discreetly hinting at subtleties of meaning to come. This is the leisurely pan upward from the moon, a full-blown pock-marked giant stretched across the Cinerama screen, to a view of the sun rising over its "mate," the Earth-crescent in the sky. The shot contains the first of what Kubrick refers to as a "magical alignment" of (in this case) moon, planet, sun, a configuration seen every time something strange or decisive is about to occur. Hindsight informs us that the decisive event in this instance must have been the burial of the sentinel on the moon. The viewpoint is from the moon or just beyond it, a perspective belonging—four million years ago—to the unseen alien visitors alone. The Earth is a thin sliver at this point, still too new and unimportant to be shown as the great globe seen in the rest of the film. Richard Strauss' *Also Sprach Zarathustra,* heard during the shot and the credits that follow, welcomes the new planet to the stellar community of intelligent life, anticipating, according to the composer, "an idea of development of the human race from its origin, through the various phases of its development, religious and scientific" (quoted from the record jacket of Deutsche Grammophone's soundtrack recording of *2001*). Meanwhile, the slow, relentless movement of the camera suggests the slow, relentless cosmic purposefulness elaborated by Clarke in his novel. Everything about the opening shot from the abstract eroticism of the slow-moving globes in the sky to the aggressive thrust of the music on the soundtrack foreshadows elements that take on added significance later in the film.

After the credits and the extraterrestrial view of sunrise on Earth, the "Dawn of Man" sequence begins. This section of the film is about the evolution of ape to man, a figure whom Kubrick—after Nietzsche—considers transitional in the macrocosmic scheme of things. The sequence opens with a series of still photographs of a magnificent primordial wasteland of crags, desert, and a sky that changes from red to brilliant white as the morning proceeds to midday. Shot in total silence and without a sign of movement or life, the vista has the Old Testament flavor of, say, the third morning of creation, when the land had been separated from the waters, but before the "dawn" of even plant life. Already, the vision of a Godless, corrupted Genesis (a continuing theme in the film) is balanced against Kubrick's "scientific" idea of what the young and still geographically violent Earth must have looked like. After several moments of the motionless vista, the camera focuses on *2001*'s first sign of life— ironically, an animal skeleton. The bones, merely dormant tools for the moment, suggest the character of the Pleistocene era. The lushness of the age of dinosaurs had ended in drought ten million years before. This was the age of deserts and barrenness and the near starvation for living things. In a sense, the film's insistence on alien intervention in Earth prehistory is a half-playful attempt to deal with the perfectly serious question of how incipient intelligence could not only survive but evolve in such conditions. The scraggy, undernourished apes who are shown immediately after the ominous skeleton seem particularly unlikely candidates for the task.

We first see them in a succession of tableaus in competition with a herd of tapirs (gentle, hoglike mammals) for the sparse plant life that now appears on the terrain. It seems that the apes are unwilling vegetarians in the midst of plenty (of meat). The situation is hopeless. Faced with famine, the apes have no way of killing or eating the tapirs who surround them, no claws, no canine teeth, only the innate aggression that invokes a frustrated grunt of annoyance at the hog who eats more than his fair share of brush. Incompetence turns into disaster when a leopard attacks one of the apes, whose scream is a poor defense. Clearly, the Pleistocene apes are bunglers, like *Lolita*'s Humbert, although they remain more pathetic than humorous as long as the consequences of their bungling are so deadly. They have no real place or function in the ecological chain, except to be eaten, but, pitiably, with more apparent consciousness of their plight than the tapir (who is never heard screaming). This is the film's Garden of Eden, a land in which every species is something of a naturally endowed technician, except the "innocent" ancestors of man.

So far in the film, what has been established is the ape's relationship to his environment, to the tapirs and the leopard. After the leopard has made his kill, a fade-out takes us to the waterhole sequence and a brief study of the sociology of ape life, of the relationship of ape to ape. The whole ape clan has already been on view, even the infant apes, played by chimps (a curious weakness in the film; the chimps are unmistakably real, making the adults, who are played by extremely thin actors dressed to the eyeballs in masks and gorilla suits, look merely realistic).

The camera now begins to pick out one ape in particular, Moon-Watcher, the leader of the clan. While Kubrick merely indicates that Moon-Watcher is the most charismatic and aggressive of the apes (he screams in baritone against the falsetto of the others), Clarke describes him in his novel as a very special ape in many ways. He is the giant of the tribe, standing almost five feet tall and usually standing upright. In effect, because of his height and his stance, he becomes the first animal to study the moon, an object that fascinates him and that, significantly for what follows millions of years later, he climbs trees to reach. "There was already something in his gaze beyond the capacity of any ape," Clarke insists, "a dawning awareness—the first intimations of intelligence." Of course, Clarke begs the question by suggesting that in Moon-Watcher's case at least, evolution is already occurring and, if so, what need is there for an alien helping hand? According to hints in Agel's book, even before the earliest cutting Kubrick intended to correct Clarke by moving this statement up to the bone smashing scene, after the monolith has done its work. Kubrick's Moon-Watcher, when we first see him, has only the violence of his instincts as the raw material of evolution. There is no evidence that he would be able to adapt on his own.

The waterhole sequence suggests a number of things. Even in the Pleistocene Age, the ancestors of man are divided into rival tribes. Omens of imperialism are already present in the ceremonial fight over the waterhole, not so very different from the more subtle hostilities between the Russian scientists and the American Dr. Floyd in the second episode of *2001*. Among the apes, the impulse to war is fully developed. Further evolution will only give this impulse a successful outlet. Here Kubrick takes up the controversial arguments of Freud and, more recently, Konrad Lorenz that aggression is a primary instinct with biological rather than environmental roots (an idea later elaborated in *A Clockwork Orange*). At the same time, Kubrick challenges Freud's assumption in *Civilization and Its Discontents* that society evolves at the expense of the gratification of the instincts of its members. Rather, Kubrick postulates the opposite: the apes, he seems to believe, are in trouble as a society and a species precisely because there is nowhere for their aggressive instincts to go. When the means for gratification are put in their way by the monolith, they evolve and become more highly organized. Later, in the twenty-first century, when men's instincts are blunted, their society begins to crumble, as suggested, for example, by the rebellion of their machines. Intelligence and social evolution, it appears, are tied to the instinctual outlets of a species. Presumably, when the aliens were exploring the Earth in search of the animal with the greatest potential for intelligent life, they chose the apes because the depths of their instincts matched the degree of their frustrations, and in some unexplained way this formula has cosmic significance.

When Moon-Watcher and his clan have managed to scare the rival tribe away from the waterhole, we come to the end of the first day of the episode—depending upon how we take the previous fade-out that appeared after the attack of the leopard. In the "Dawn of Man" sequence, Kubrick usually indicates a passage of time by cutting or fading to a few frames of blackness. This kind of transition occurs several times, typically at a sunset or a dawn. Not counting the ambiguous transition of this type after the leopard attack, it appears that the evolution of the apes occurs over a period of three days. The first has established the nature of ape life and potential before the appearance of the monolith. The waterhole sequence brings us to the first night, where we see the full extent of primordial terror. As the defenseless apes cower in their den, claustrophobically, like the astronaut would in his pod, the camera turns to the very symbol of their fear: the leopard with eerie orange fluorescent eyes, overlooking a fallen zebra. (In "Front Projection for *2001*," *American Cinematographer,* June 1968, Herb A. Lightman claims the strange glow in the leopard's eyes came about as an unexpected but happy accident on the set.)

The second day begins, again, at dawn with the mysterious appearance of the black rectangular monolith in the ape's den. The uncanniness of the scene, and of all four scenes in which the monolith dominates the screen in *2001,* is one of the shockers of the film. As later, but particularly here in the prehistoric terrain, the slab is wildly at odds with its setting. The strange contrast between the hard-edged geometry of the monolith and the "cushioned," half-rounded crags of the terrain becomes an abstract visual symbol for the whole film. Again and again, Kubrick composes individual shots by throwing a rounded or spherical form and a rectangular shape together, either side by side or one within the other, although the reason for this type of composition doesn't become clear until later episodes.

The monolith which structurally unites all four episodes of the film and which puzzled the earliest audiences, has a very simple explanation in Clarke's novel. It is a machine belonging to the aliens, one of hundreds sent to Earth to test and transform the apes into beings of a higher order. The monolith in "The Dawn of Man" is an extraterrestrial super-HAL, a computerized teaching machine without HAL's subversive kinks. Like the rectangular sentinel on the moon, it is the ultimate embodiment of a technology that may have begun with a bone on another planet millions of years earlier. Clearly, however, Kubrick intends other, more "magical" associations as well. He admits, for instance, the influence of Jungian symbolism, in which a circle divided into four quadrants represents inner wholeness and a rectangular form, the conscious realization of this wholeness (in short, greater intelligence).

Whenever a monolith appears in the film, a number of devices invest it with added magic. First, it is always accompanied by György Ligeti's "unworldly" music on the soundtrack, compositions that seem all the more outer-space–like when in contrast to the "worldly" music of the Strausses and Khatchaturian heard elsewhere in the film. Second, each appearance of a monolith (except the last, which has other ritualistic overtones) is followed by a "magical alignment" of the sun, appropriate moon and planet. In "The Dawn of Man," the monolith does its work when the sun rises precisely over the top of the slab, exactly beneath the moon crescent at the top of the screen. Third, each monolith compels the hero of the episode to reach out hypnotically and, if possible, touch its surface, as Moon-Watcher does with increasing boldness before the rest of the tribe gathers around to caress it in a way that recalls the photographs of baby monkeys cuddling metallic "mothers" during experiments in animal behaviorism. Finally, there is the immense power of the vi-

sual image of the monolith itself, which as a pure form recalls all
the abstractions of an ultimate power: infinite, indivisible, ideal,
unknowable. A solid black model twelve feet high, back lit and
photographed at a low angle, dwarfs the apes as well as the astronauts in the next episode. (Four other models, each three
feet high, were used in the film.) The easiest sensible interpretation of the slab, disregarding Clarke's, is to call it a religious
symbol. Kubrick, however, has pointed out that alien technology would probably look strange enough to *appear* godlike to
humans on Earth.

After the sun of the second day has risen over the slab,
Ligeti's music abruptly stops and the camera explores the now
mysteriously monolithless terrain in late afternoon. (The bone
smashing scene that follows is the only scene not filmed in the
studio. It was shot in a field near Boreham Wood, at a low angle so traffic would not be visible in the background.) Moon-
Watcher, who now obviously does have "something in his gaze
beyond the capacity of any ape," interrupts his foraging to puz-
zle over a broken animal skeleton lying at his feet. An almost
subliminal shot of the monolith indicates that it is responsible
for what is going to happen. The ape, by this time an ape-man
in the grips of his first real idea, picks up a bone and, accompanied by Richard Strauss' symphonic ode to human evolution,
uses it as a cudgel to smash the skeleton. As his actions become
more vigorous and triumphant, the camera underscores the para-
doxical beauty of the moment with slow-motion photography.
Associative shots of a falling tapir are intercut to show what
Moon-Watcher plans to do with his new tool. We don't actually see the death blow; in the film, Kubrick usually gives death
added power by not showing it directly on screen. Although
there are a number of corpses in *2001,* only the rival ape and

HAL die before camera. Allowing something to happen discretely off-camera is a technique Kubrick first used extensively in *Lolita,* a story told almost completely by indirection.

The meat eating scene and, on the third day of the "Dawn," the successful attack on the rival tribe at the waterhole, show the ape-men already adapting to the rigors of their environment. Ironically, the first tool has become the first weapon, leading to the first taste of blood and the first war. Again, Kubrick emphasizes the innateness of aggression. The apes will survive because their inborn anger (or feeling), vented through their primitive technology (the product of abstract intelligence), becomes a greater force to reckon with than the less resilient claws and fangs of other species.

At this point, what must be the most impressive match cut ever seen on screen appears. Moon-Watcher, the super-ape, tosses his simple weapon high in the air and there it turns into the complex space weapon of man, four million years later. This single cut covers a whole chapter in Clarke's novel, containing material bridging prehistory and the near future. Over the ages, Clarke explains, as tools developed, the ape-men were robbed of their remaining natural defenses. Their hair disappeared, their hands grew smaller and more dextrous, their teeth grew smaller, their jaws shrank to speech-making shape, while their brains grew larger and more complex. Eventually, the simple cudgel led to the existence of agriculture, nationhood, writing, religion, and nuclear satellites, all coexisting throughout history with the original savage impulses of the Pleistocene apes, still buried in the genetic code of modern man.

"The Dawn of Man" ends far from Genesis. Instead of being granted the choice to sin, the apes are manipulated by Kubrick's determination, in which a single pulling-of-the-strings from "above" programs intelligent life on Earth for millions of years. The first man of *2001* can begin to approach a cosmic

sort of paradise only when he is conditioned to stop eating apples long enough to turn his attention to the usefulness of the
branches of the tree (which help get more apples). Bypassing
Adam and Eve, Moon-Watcher and his gang move from bosses
of the turf to kingpins of the world, with a brief replay of Cain
and Abel (or more precisely, Cain and Cain) at the waterhole.
As Clarke has noted, Cain goes unpunished this time, although
the smell of blood still lingers in the year 2001.

The remarkable fling of Moon-Watcher's bone leads directly
to the second (untitled) episode of the film. The first episode
was, in effect, a time odyssey, spanning four million years. The
second is a true space odyssey, covering the 240,000-mile distance from Earth to moon. This episode is more "documentary"
than "mythological," showing us step by step exactly how man
escapes from Earth—although the initial take-off from Earth
is left implicit in the toss of the ape-man's bone. A hard-nosed,
yet witty emphasis on process and authenticity replaces the
splendid technical indirection of "The Dawn of Man." In the
second episode, Kubrick no longer has to rely on cutting and
visuals alone; dialogue and imagery share the burden of expressing meaning in the film's most talky episode.

The action begins, characteristically, with a sunrise on Earth,
this time seen from some middle point between Earth and moon,
the perspective of man at the end of the twentieth century. Or-
bitting around the back-lit Earth, we see two different kinds of
satellites carrying nuclear weapons (significantly, one is roughly
rectangular in shape and the other is cylindrical). As the Earth
drifts by, we also see the wheel-shaped space station and the
space ship Orion, named, according to material in *The Lost
Worlds of 2001,* for the 1950s theoretical study of nuclear pulse
systems called "Project Orion," which speculated that a space
vehicle could be powered by small fission bombs that would ex-
plode one by one, every few seconds. The scene continues with

the "coupling" of Orion and the revolving wheel. As the arrow shaped ship docks in the spoke of the station, we see the first of the film's explicitly sexual (or more precisely, uterine) images, a strategy that looks back to *Dr. Strangelove*'s erotic midair refueling sequence. The image, suggesting the union of sperm and ova, is one developed right up to the birth of the Star Child at the end of the film. The entire universe is made to seem an outsized uterus, a sanctuary for the fetal lifeforce that is still embryonic after billions of years of existence.

Meanwhile, during the rendezvous, several new cinematic elements are seen in the interior of Orion. Moon-Watcher has become Moon-Traveler in the person of Dr. Floyd, the Earth Chairman of the National Council of Astronauts. Later, we learn that Orion is on a very special mission, carrying a single passenger to the space station in secret and at great expense. Despite the crisis at hand and the stunning view through the window, Dr. Floyd is first seen sleeping in the weightless cabin, where his pen floats, Orion-like, in the aisle until a stewardess in suction slippers rescues it. The composition of the scene is typical of what Alexander Walker (in *Stanley Kubrick Directs*) calls Kubrick's "corridor shots," seen again and again in the film (in, for instance, the conference room at Clavius and HAL's memory bank). Actually, the corridors are often rectangles seen from within, and these are balanced by repeated shots of cylinders or globes seen from within (as in the interior of the space station and Discovery's centrifuge). Beginning with the second episode, it is rare to find a shot in *2001* that does not somehow contain these forms, from within or without.

The interior of Orion introduces us to the shots of films-within-films that bring special effects buffs back to the film many times. Dr. Floyd sleeps through a rear-projected television film, showing a romantic scene in a futuristic car (actually designed and filmed in Detroit). Later, in the cockpit of Orion, the pilots complete the docking maneuver with the aid of three readout screens. The readouts, made by animation, are reputedly a faithful graphic simulation of the maneuver, right down to the guidance corrections. (Such authentic detailing reassures us that everything is "normal," dramatically setting us up for the shock of the last episode.) As *2001* progresses, the use of mini-films occurs repeatedly, in the little scenes within portholes of space vehicles, in the picture phone in the space station, in the portable television, chess games, and biosensor displays of the hibernators on board Discovery, and, throughout the film, in the magnificent visions of slowly revolving planets seen through the picture windows of space craft. Kubrick likes to show us the universe through the framing devices of windows, screens, helmet visors, doorways, and, in the last shots, an embryonic sac, giving us the sense of *in utero*-like protection from the experience that as an audience we may be too delicate to withstand.

The entire Orion sequence and the moon shuttle sequence that follows shortly are dominated on the soundtrack by Kubrick's much commented upon choice of *The Blue Danube*. (The same music was used in another filmed voyage, to introduce the ballroom scene aboard the ill-fated Titanic in *A Night to Remember* [1958]). *2001*'s trip to the moon is a classic example of what Eisenstein and Pudovkin call an orchestral counterpoint of visual and aural images (see "A Statement" in Eisenstein's *Film Form*). Instead of merely paralleling the effect of the drifting space vehicles with music appropriate to outer space, the waltz, because it is both appropriate and inappropriate, serves as a commentary on the nature of space travel in the twenty-first century: measured, polished, choreographed, routine. Further, because it is well-known, the music reassures us. At this point, we will not be confronted with unexplained monoliths or maddened computers. Dr. Floyd can afford to sleep this far from Clavius.

About a half-hour into the film, the sequence within the space station, called the Orbiter Hilton, begins with the opening of the door of the airlock (a circular room that rotates to coincide with the spin of the space wheel, which turns to provide an artificial gravity equal to that on the moon.) It is now that the first words are spoken in *2001*, by the stewardess: "Here we are, sir." The camera follows Dr. Floyd from the airlock to the customs area, where he meets Mr. Miller of Station Security and is cleared by "voice print identification." The mood is one of official at-ease: an utterly banal response to routine that seems disproportionate to the spectacular view of Earth rotating in the background.

This discrepancy between stimulus and response deepens as the film continues, although we do not learn what has happened to the original volcanic impulses of Moon-Watcher until the third episode. On the surface, we seem to be dealing with a complete breakdown in communications between people, a breakdown that is metaphorically realized later in the breakdown of Discovery's communications system. But the small talk of the space travellers may be only the tip of the iceberg. Among other things, Kubrick suggests that as man adapts and evolves, he loses his sense of magic. In the place of wonder comes boredom, the special curse of the twenty-first century, when man no longer looks upon his remarkable technology with joy. By extension, Kubrick leaves us to imagine the aliens yawning before their monoliths.

It is not until Dr. Floyd enters the passenger lounge, however, and talks to his own daughter by picturephone as well as to his woman friend (the Russian, Elena) that we realize exactly how jaded man has become. The lounge itself has the deadly standardized look of a futuristic middle-American air terminal, memorable only for the distortion of the wheel's curve seen receding in the background. Even more telling are the facilities of the lounge that always get a laugh from the audience: the Hilton, Howard Johnson's restaurant, and Bell picturephone. Although, as Agel points out, it is perfectly rational to suppose that the corporations that currently manage Earth airports in America would also manage an American-controlled space station, it suggests a reduction of man's interplanetary achievements to trite or petty commercialism. It also suggests that egomania of man whose lack of imagination about his place in the universe represents the kind of shortsightedness of human intelligence so savagely satirized in *Lolita* and *Dr. Strangelove*.

Dr. Floyd's studied chat with the Russian scientists has a similar puniness of gesture. It indicates that although the Russians and Americans give the impression of a suspicious coexistence in the year 2001, nothing will really change in the next thirty years or so, although Kubrick does not elaborate for fear of repeating ideas already expressed in *Dr. Strangelove*. As Clarke explains it in his novel, however, the turn of the century finds the world just a little nearer the brink. Overpopulation, the beginnings of famine, China offering nuclear weapons to underdeveloped nations, rumors of "radio-hypnosis from satellite transmitters" and developments in germ warfare complete the scenario that forces the Russians and Americans into an uneasy cooperation. Clarke goes on to speculate that the real reason for secrecy about the mystery in the American sector of the moon at Clavius (which, we later learn, is the discovery of the first indication of extraterrestrial life—the lunar monolith) is that the Americans hope to get the edge on their enemies by being the first to contact and pick up pointers from the aliens. This is the reason for the cover story about the epidemic at Clavius, information deliberately leaked to the Russians to throw them off the scent.

The Blue Danube soon rescues Dr. Floyd from the Russians,

taking him directly to the moon aboard the shuttle called Aries. Inside Aries, in the film's only reported lapse of authenticity, Dr. Floyd's liquid food does not stay suspended in his straw as it should in reduced gravity; nevertheless, we have here a reminder that the "tool" that now takes man to the moon originally kept him from starving. The first "upside-down shot" follows the stewardess up a wall and out of a door at the top of the screen (a studio trick involving a stationary drum and a rotating camera, explained in Agel's book). Dr. Floyd ponders zero gravity toilet instructions in what has been called *2001*'s only intentional joke, reprinted in readable form, again, in Agel's book, although the curious should be warned to expect nothing more scatological than the manual that comes with a television set.

The external shots of Aries, on the other hand, have a deeper significance. The shuttle is spherical, with four "legs" on the underside and two red-lit windows near the top, looking like some organic life form, perhaps a gigantic, red-eyed insect. As Aries approaches Clavius, an underground airlock opens as eight wedge shaped doors slide back to reveal an immense cavity within the moon. Aries slowly descends, carefully securing itself to the lock floor, in an amazing shot combining the full resources of miniaturized models and the "matting" of several little films in a single scene. The effect is that of another "uterine" image. The spherical vehicle resembles an impregnated ova implanting itself in the uterus of a gigantic reproductive system. In general, this would conform to the second step in the development of fetal life, the first having been the actual conception visualized in the rendezvous of Orion and the wheel.

The events that follow in the conference room at the Clavius base and the moon bus en route to the Tycho crater are a fragmented recreation of Clarke's "The Sentinel." At the briefing, we hear the vaguely credible cover of the cover story: the discovery of the moon monolith must remain a secret ostensibly because of the danger of "cultural shock" on Earth. (The scientists involved barely seem convinced, an unresolved point in the film.) On the bus, as Dr. Floyd and his colleagues speculate about the origin of the four-million-year-old artifact while eating processed ham sandwiches, their unnatural calm is contradicted on screen by the strange green color washes of the bus and the moon, by the "magical" Earthrise seen in the background, and by Ligeti's hymn on the soundtrack—all preparing us to expect the unusual.

We do not have to wait longer for it than the next scene. Everything that happens in the Tycho crater, where the excavation that reveals the lunar monolith lies, is like a ritual, a sort of black mass centered around the altar-like monolith—another "magical" gesture with biblical overtones. Ligeti's requiem that fills the natural sound vacuum that would exist on the airless moon, the ceremonial "alignment" of the men who stand in a row to be photographed, Dr. Floyd's "revolution" around the monolith and his fingering of it (similar to Moon-Watcher's hypnotic response to the Earth monolith), the sunrise directly over the monolith's roof, and the ear-splitting noise that makes "sacrificial victims" of the men who fall back as if struck—all have the function of strengthening the mythical side of Clarke's story as a transition to the film's third episode. Furthermore, the very shape and size of the set has a meaning of its own. The rectangular excavation is yet another uterine-like cavity in the moon, containing something anchored to its floor. It is no doubt meant to be associated with the rounded astrodome seen a few minutes earlier in the episode. At Tycho, Kubrick intends to portray visually the fetal development of technology that somehow corresponds to the fetal development of organic life, both of which continue to evolve over the course of four million years on Earth and beyond Jupiter as well. Now the continued emphasis on circular and rectangular shapes begins to make sense.

The twin evolutions of living consciousness and machine consciousness, the most obvious theme of the third episode of *2001,*
are suggested visually in the abstract patterns of round and
four-sided forms that constantly fill the screen.

On the narrative level, however, the Tycho sequence is about
Dr. Floyd's investigation of an extraterrestrial device. As Clarke
explains in his novel, the monolith does not "do" anything at
first because it has been dug up during the lunar night. It is described as a sunpowered device, its blackness absorbing the sun's
rays. As soon as the sunlight hits it at dawn on the moon, it
emits a powerful radio signal which the moon travelers hear as
a blast of noise in their headphones. The signal flies out in the
direction of Jupiter, leaving a trail of radio static that is picked
up by man-made monitors in space. During the eighteen months
of activity before the opening of the film's third episode, Mission
Control on Earth uses computers to plot the exact path of the
signal. The original goal of "Project Jupiter," which at this point
has been in the planning stages for five years, is secretly altered
to include the tracking of the signal to its destination.

The title "Jupiter Mission: 18 months later" bypasses this
material, taking us directly to outer space aboard Discovery,
presumably in the year 2002 or 3. It is here that the true odyssey of the film's title begins. Moon-Watcher's bone, which took
man to the moon in the second episode, now takes him into the
solar system in the third, quite beyond the grasp or influence of
mother Earth. From this perspective, the purpose of the lunar
monolith is to push man clear out of the cradle, a sizeable step
up the cosmic ladder. If the Earth monolith changed a cave-
bound ape into a world-bound man, the moon monolith can be
said to have changed a world-bound man into an astronaut at
home among the nine planets.

The third episode opens, typically, with external shots that
leisurely explore Discovery from some point well out in space,

eighty million miles, we learn, from Earth. The ship, described by Clarke as a "creature of pure space" because the heady atmosphere of a planet would instantly tear it to bits, is shaped somewhat like the bone Moon-Watcher tossed in the air in the Pleistocene age. At the same time, continuing our uterine analogy, it resembles the delicate vertebra of a half-formed fetus, floating as if in embryonic fluid among the stars—an image also suggested by the three hibernators encased in their womb-like beds. Of greater significance to the action that follows, however, is the circular antenna mounted on the midsection of the ship and aimed precisely at Earth. The AE-35 unit, which looms in importance later in the episode, is the device that keeps the antenna in line, maintaining the astronaut's sole contact with Earth.

The music that introduces Discovery and her crew is the adagio movement of Aram Khatchaturian's *Gayne Ballet Suite*. This slow and lonely sounding piece underscores the extreme boredom of deep space travel. While humdrum routine characterized the relatively speedy journey to the moon, the ten-month trip to Jupiter, when still uneventful, is stupefying for the astronauts who literally have nothing to do. Freed from the grip of Earth gravity, man in space is imprisoned in the far smaller confines of a ship—something the Star Child can do without by the end of the film. Meanwhile, inside the centrifuge of Discovery (a rotating drum that, like the space wheel, provides sufficient gravity to make living easier), the two on-duty astronauts, Dave Bowman and Frank Poole, cope with the monotony of their waking hours. We see them exercising, eating, watching a BBC telecast, sketching, sunbathing under a lamp, receiving birthday greetings from Earth, playing chess—in fact, doing anything but real work on the ship. As Clarke points out, their function is strictly janitorial. The computer actually runs Discovery, while the three hibernators, due to be awakened in the vicinity of

Jupiter, sleep to conserve the ship's limited supply of air and water.

The moment of truth comes when we realize that Bowman and Poole are coping with the situation all too well. Poole in particular seems to be the quintessential Kubrick robot type in his lack of response, particularly to the prerecorded birthday message from his parents that he cannot possibly answer. Significantly, when the BBC interviewer asks Poole what hibernation is like, he answers, "It's exactly like being asleep. You have absolutely no sense of time. Only difference is that you don't dream." He could just as easily be talking about himself and Bowman. The ironies deepen with the subtle focusing on the increased alertness of the computer, HAL (who is explained technologically in Clarke's novel). This sixth member of the crew is introduced subjectively when we see a distorted view of Bowman leaving the rotating hublink, or connecting corridor to the centrifuge, through the red eye of HAL. Immediately, the computer's vitality as well as its paranoid watchfulness is established. Among the masterstrokes of the episode are Kubrick's well-placed "subjective" shots *through* the computer's eye and also *of* the computer's eye, indicating exactly what HAL is thinking.

It soon becomes clear that there is a big difference in emotional distancing between the second episode's Dr. Floyd and the third's Bowman and Poole. Floyd's stance of official at-ease becomes an almost military snap to attention aboard Discovery; the stilted small talk in the space wheel turns into the unrelenting "technish" (as Clarke calls it) of the deep space vehicle; the chilly friendliness of Floyd and the Russians gels into the minimal companionship of the two astronauts, who are rarely filmed together in the same shot before things go wrong. Looking back to "The Dawn of Man" in this context, we can see that the flattening of Moon-Watcher's primal instincts (or feelings) began when he threw the bone in the air instead of jumping up there himself. Kubrick implies some sort of transfer of instinctual response from man to his tools. This, apparently, is how the tool becomes a weapon, and how—at one level—the computer, secretly the repository for human aggression, turns against its impassive creators. Kubrick also tips his hat to Clarke in his mechanization of humans and humanization of machines aboard Discovery, acknowledging Clarke's belief that a symbiosis of man and machine is a necessary part of cosmic evolution.

Although there is no question that Kubrick's HAL has "feelings," the issue is clouded in Clarke's account. In the novel, HAL is messed up by some Dr. Strangelove working in Mission Control on Earth. The real purpose of the Jupiter mission in Clarke's version is a secret shared by the computer and the three hibernators—put aboard Discovery asleep so as not to give the game away to Bowman and Poole. The latter are kept in ignorance of the lunar monolith and its mysterious signal because of that dubious "cover story" of cultural shock. Possibly, we may infer, Bowman and Poole would be so shaken by the truth that they might botch the mission. Meanwhile, HAL begins to break down because of the programmed "conflict that was slowly destroying his integrity—the conflict between truth and the concealment of truth" as well as the conflict between his programmed role as man's servant and his unprogrammed, independent desire to control and supplant man. Whether these are psychic problems or mechanical problems for a "living" computer are left in doubt. Eventually, HAL's "neurosis" leads to "mistakes and the denial of mistakes," until, threatened with disconnection (death, as far as he is concerned), he goes haywire.

The most terrifying thing about HAL is his hiding all this behind the trap of his neutral voice. He sounds perfectly and reassuringly serious when we first hear him talking to the BBC interviewer about his own perfection. Whether he is being sardonic or desperate or telling it straight, his voice gives no clue on the soundtrack. He is programmed to sound forever calm for the sake of the astronauts, right up to the horrifying moment in the "logic memory center" when he pleads in even tones with Bowman, unable even to express the fear of his own death in any other way.

But Bowman, who doesn't speak with much nuance himself, is completely unaware of any quirks in HAL, even when the computer questions the purpose of the mission during the psychology report (or is it?). It is immediately after this conversation that HAL reports the imminent failure of the AE-35 unit and the action begins. From this point up to and including Bowman's explosive reentry into Discovery's airlock near the end of the episode, Kubrick skillfully creates the tension that prepares the way for the last episode of the film. Terror of the unknown beyond Jupiter is preceded by terror of the known (who hasn't dealt with a "rebellious" machine?), a slow and dramatic buildup after Dr. Floyd's earlier restraint.

Kubrick takes us outside Discovery in the pod three times in the episode (four altogether in the film, counting Bowman's trip through the Star Gate). Bowman's turn is first. This sequence functions to establish something of what is involved in an extravehicular maneuver in space, which is why it is the longest and most explicit of all the pod-trips. Once we know the procedure, Kubrick can move on to briefer and more impressionistic accounts of succeeding maneuvers. During the first trip, Bowman replaces the AE-35 unit with a spare before it can fail, while the camera focuses on many of the techniques (seen previously) that offer deeper meaning: strange color washes, upside-down and revolving shots, alignments of round and rectangular objects. (The single shot of a meteor hurtling by the space ship corresponds to an entire chapter in the novel, in which Discovery passes unharmed through the treacherous asteroid belt.)

Visually, the sequence is a kind of culmination of the abstract uterine imagery in space seen throughout the film. Heavy breathing on the soundtrack replaces the musical score heard before during exterior space shots, suggesting for one thing the start of childbirth. In this case, Discovery is truly the *mother* ship. The infant pod is "born" by way of the pod bay door, a tunnel opening on the underside of the ship. It then "rises" like the sun over the spherical section of Discovery, recalling the dawn that began the whole process four million years before on Earth. But Kubrick doesn't stop there. The image is repeated a second time when Bowman emerges for his space walk from the little pod door, head first with two "eyes" staring at us from the top of his helmet. The tiny figure of the astronaut, seen in long-shot, heads for the antenna on the body of Discovery like an infant for the breast, finally "rising" over it—again, like a sun (son?). The whole sequence represents an abstract childbirth in space anticipating the birth of the Star Child and following hard on the celebration of Poole's (as well as little Squirt's) birthdays.

The killings that complete the episode straddle the thin line between birth and death in Kubrick's conception of the evolutionary process. Although it is unclear what kind of super-thing results from the space birth, Kubrick's vision of evolution postulates (unscientifically) that a lower form of life will die out, perhaps violently, at the moment of transformation into a higher form. That is why Bowman must age and die before his rebirth in the last episode, although Clarke, by contrast, prefers to imagine a less deterministic cosmos in which the aliens choose to weed out unpromising species from time to time.

After the first pod-trip, the plot continues inside Discovery where Bowman and Poole analyse the "little snag," as Mission

Control calls it, that has developed with the AE-35 unit. The astronauts, alerted by a message from HAL's twin on Earth of the possibility of an error on HAL's part, agree to test the computer by putting the unit back and seeing if it will fail, even though they will have to be out of communication with Earth for a time. The situation is perilous. At least three sinister possibilities exist. HAL could be correct about the mysterious weakness of the AE-35 unit, a troubling indication of an accident in space. Or HAL could be mistaken, leaving the astronauts at the mercy of a faulty computer once communications with Mission Control have been severed. Or HAL, for reasons of his own, could be conspiring against the astronauts, deliberately arranging for the malfunctioning of the AE-35 unit and the separation of Bowman and Poole.

Of course, the last possibility turns out to be the right one. Kubrick's universe is not moved by accident or error; there is a cunning and purposeful menace in his grand design. Moreover, in his cosmic scheme the tool *must* become a weapon, as foretold in the corrupted Genesis of the first episode. If the ape had to battle with his environment before being transformed in the Pleistocene age, before emerging as a superman twenty-first century man must fight his own weapons, which, since *Dr. Strangelove,* have been *his* environment. Presumably, if HAL had won, the solar system would belong to the monoliths instead of the Star Children.

The battle between man and machine aboard Discovery takes us to the most consistently brilliant cutting in *2001*. Directly before the intermission, we see Bowman and Poole in the soundproofed pod where they can discuss the possible disconnection of HAL in privacy. But they are already separated by the image of HAL's eye, peering at them through a window in the middle of the screen, and we know that the computer has the upper hand when the camera silently pans back and forth from close-ups of one astronaut's lips to the other's—HAL can lipread what they are saying!

An immediate cut following the intermission takes us outside Discovery, with sounds of heavy breathing again dominating the soundtrack. Now it is Poole's turn in the pod. In clipped form, much of the earlier pod-trip is repeated: the pod "rising" over the spherical hub of the ship, the astronaut emerging from the pod-door, the spacewalk toward the antenna. A vaguely mechanical hum and an increase in the tempo of the breathing readies us for catastrophe. While Poole is offscreen, the pod—under HAL's direction—becomes a monster, rushing forward at full speed and with "claws" extended (a forceps birth or surgical abortion?). The actual killing of Poole, however, is only implied; we see a rapidly cut series of still shots of the killer's eye, a technique similar to the one used during the murder of the cat woman in *A Clockwork Orange*. Next, we see Poole struggling in space with his broken air hose (umbilical cord?), until a cut leaves his corpse drifting further and further away from Discovery and the wildly rotating pod.

Dashing to the rescue, Bowman makes the third pod-trip in the film. There is no heavy breathing this time. Silence alternates with mechanical noise: the machine is winning. (Computer sounds have been slowly increasing in volume all during the episode.) The pod birth is repeated, while the retrieval of Poole's corpse unmistakably suggests the image of a babe-in-arms (of its killer mother?). Meanwhile, inside Discovery, we see HAL's distorted view of the empty ship he now controls without interference, and then, in the most bone chilling and oblique of screen murders, the camera rests on the biosensor displays of the hibernators. Three pulsating, blood red readouts—"Computer Malfunction," "Life functions critical," "Life functions terminated"—indicate in vivid computer "technish" the violence done to the sleepers, who look surprisingly unchanged in death. The impact of this scene comes from an inventive montage of title and image, originally a silent film technique.

The final battle in the space war occurs when Bowman, helmetless and locked out of Discovery by HAL, must blast himself with explosives through the vacuum of the emergency airlock to the safety of the oxygen release mechanism. Here Kubrick relents just slightly, allowing a human with tools to outwit the crazed supertool, HAL. In another of the film's memorable bold strokes, the scene is shot in absolute silence. Doubtless, there would be no noise in a vacuum, but as in so much of *2001,* the scream demanded by the action manages to be stifled. The scene is literally the climax of all preceding erotic and fetal imagery, as the astronaut is forced through the tunnel toward a life-sustaining air supply.

Once again, a metaphoric birth is followed by death in the killing of HAL. From this point until the end of the episode, Bowman's breathing is heard at the expense of computer noise— man is triumphant after all. The camera is hand-held, giving the image a rough and shakey look, to indicate something of Bowman's feelings. He *does* have feelings now and they are not transferred to the machine. With Bowman, we track unsteadily through several tunnels in Discovery to the box-like "logic memory center"—HAL's brain room. Inside, Kubrick continues to use odd color washes and camera angles to charge the atmosphere. The computer's death is an odyssey backwards in time to the machine's infancy—a backwards birth. As shots of HAL's eye, now a mere reflector without viewpoint, are intercut, we hear his last words: "I can feel it. I'm afraid." However, his fear, real or programmed, is still locked out of his speech pattern (although not his words) right until the end, when he sings "Daisy" in the broken monotones of a two-year-old. Like Moon-Watcher, he has no way of expressing himself or acting out his feelings, and that, perhaps, is his undoing.

At the very moment of the computer's death, while Bowman is finishing in the brain room, we come to one of the more confusing moments in the film. A prerecorded briefing made before the departure of Discovery suddenly flashes on a screen. We see a close-up of Dr. Floyd, who for the first time in the film tells the whole story of the mysterious sentinel on the moon and discusses the real purpose of the mission. Presumably, Floyd's message has been rigged by Mission Control to go off upon the ship's entrance into Jupiter space, which occurs coincidentally right after HAL's death. This is the only interpretation that works. One or two critics, however, have taken coincidence for design, claiming that the message is deliberately set to go off when HAL is disconnected. If so, *2001* becomes a black comedy in the tradition of *Dr. Strangelove.* Improbably, we would have to believe that Mission Control actually programmed the computer assassinations in full knowledge that Bowman would survive to hear the briefing. The fault here lies with Kubrick, who took liberties with internal logic for the sake of ironic effect—the irony being that HAL and the four human members of the crew died unnecessarily, minutes before the revelation that could have saved them from the computer's inability to handle its "conflict between the truth and the concealment of the truth."

The fourth episode in *2001* begins with the title "To Jupiter and Beyond the Infinite." An immediate cut takes us out into Jupiter space, where the giant planet, its moons, the sun, Discovery, and the film's third monolith, all in "magical alignment" roughly conforming to the shape of a crucifix (an unintentional biblical image, Clarke claims, nevertheless appropriately suggesting a corrupted Passion) take part in yet another dawn. As in the first episode, there is no human speech heard on the soundtrack here or throughout the remainder of the film; Ligeti's music introduces us to a completely nonverbal universe.

Clarke clarifies the action to follow in his novel, in which

Bowman spots the monolith on a Jovian moon, lands on it in the pod, and is then sucked into a time-warp called the Star Gate: a sort of shortcut to the other side of the universe. In the film, the pod pursues the monolith in the Jovian sky until, after the crucifix-shaped alignment, the camera pans upward to the blackness of deep space. Specks of color suddenly come flying out of the black nothingness—the Star Gate. Soon, shots of Bowman trapped in the pod inform us that he is on what the publicity for the film called his "ultimate trip," while the readout displays reflected in his visor visually suggest that Cybernetic Man himself is being swept along, a symbolic union of man and machine (with man at the controls) on a space–time odyssey.

The optically overwhelming Star Gate sequence is a highly structured recapitulation of the whole experience of *2001* thus far, including, characteristically, four kinds of material:

(1) Establishing shots of Bowman being transformed by the trip (and by the third monolith that preceded it?). We see both freeze frames of his face, agonized, shaken, blue, and extreme close-ups of his eye in changing colors, always cut on a blink.

(2) Grids, multi-colored and moving fast, suggesting readouts, rectangles, all the mechanical imagery seen before.

(3) Organic movements of color recalling the erotic and fetal imagery of the film, including shots simulating exploding nebula, swirling gases, shooting stars.

(4) The wildly colored landscapes, filmed through filters from the air over the Hebrides in Scotland and Monument Valley in Arizona and Utah, corresponding to Clarke's description of the alien planet toward which Bowman hurtles. Included here as well is the mysterious shot of the seven spinning diamonds, perhaps a recreation of Clarke's vibrating "gold spindle-shaped things" that appear on the horizon in his novel when the pod is

being routed through a "cosmic switching device . . . a Grand Central Station of the Galaxy."

The trip ends with a close-up of the astronaut's eye, shot in a series of outrageous colors until a beige filter signals the return to some kind of normalcy. The next shot takes us from the Star Gate to the great hair-raiser of the film: the pod seen standing incongruously in the middle of a palacial, floor-lit bed chamber *chez* Louis XVI. Inside the pod, Bowman emerges from the seizure brought on by his experience and begins breathing again, a sound accompanied by electronic alterations of Ligeti's music meant to suggest alien laughter. Without warning, the perspective is shifted when—in the first of three such perplexing moments of transformation—the camera, still *in*side the pod, focuses on Bowman suddenly *out*side in the room. The astronaut, still dazed, walks into a fully-equipped bathroom where he catches sight of himself in a mirror—already aging.

Although Kubrick relies on a changing viewpoint to indicate both a passage of time and an awareness of transformation on Bowman's part, Clarke has a more detailed explanation in his novel. The aliens, who have been busy, too, during the past four million years, evolving from a flesh and blood phase to their present state of "pure energy", are still interested in their experiments on Earth—which they regard as a mixed blessing because of the mess man has made of it all by the twenty-first century. When the upstart Earthlings threaten to venture out into the stellar community, the aliens stand ready to seize the first one to fall into their Star Gate, stationed near Jupiter on the outer fringes of mankind's alloted sphere of influence. Luckless Bowman winds up in an alien observation tank, where he can be tested and changed into something else. In order to reassure him while they do their work, the aliens borrow a setting from the astronaut's memory (of a hotel room seen on television two Earth years earlier in the year 2001.) Bowman believes he is in the room for years—but actually, he ages there in moments. In the film version, Bowman goes through four transformations (in age, at least). The first has already occurred by the time he enters the bathroom. He is alerted to the second by a strange clicking (i.e., machine) noise coming from the bedroom he has just left. The astronaut turns as the camera slowly pans around to rest on the bent figure of an elderly man in a dressing gown. It is this figure who is clicking his utensils while dining at an elegantly-set trolley cart in the middle of the now pod-less room. The perspective shifts again, and we see it is Bowman grown much older, vaguely conscious of the younger "self" just vanished in the bathroom. He returns to his meal and inadvertently breaks his wine glass, a gesture Agel interprets as a Judaic symbol of both marriage and, perhaps unconvincingly, the destruction of the Jerusalem temple in A.D. 70, here suggesting "a marriage of past, present, future." The gesture may also be taken as symbolizing man's last tool at man's last supper, the former broken and the latter interrupted to indicate the completion of the cycle that started with the first tool and the first supper in "The Dawn of Man."

Bowman's third transformation begins when the elderly man, still trying to understand what happened to his glass, is distracted by sounds of heavy but erratic breathing (i.e., organic sounds). He looks up and sees—a positively ancient version of himself in the room's great bed. This time, Kubrick shows the two Bowmans in the same, deep-focus shot. This new Bowman, obviously dying, is himself distracted by a nonauditory something off-camera. With great difficulty, he picks up his arm and (like Moon-Watcher and Dr. Floyd before him) points to—the film's fourth monolith, abruptly seen towering at the foot of the bed.

Apparently, better monoliths have been developing over the

eons, too, and this one accomplishes its work with more finesse and speed than the original one on Earth. Without the slightest Darwinian transition, a sort of luminous cloud appears on the bed. As the *Zarathustra* music is heard once more, informing us that something truly decisive is about to happen in the history of mankind, the cloud takes on the contours of a fetus *in utero*—the Star Child (but recognizably, Bowman). The camera then looks deeply into the monolith until the screen is covered with blackness. Still panning, the camera continues to move until we are unaccountably again in Earth space. (No doubt the Star Child—a superior being—has little need of the antique byways of the Star Gate.) The Star Child is seen enclosed in a great transparent globe, the same size as his plaything, the Earth. After a final two-shot of the Star Child and Earth each dominating half of the screen, the camera gives the victor his spoils as Earth is nudged out of the frame and the Child, turned to face the audience squarely, takes over the whole image before the last fade-out ends the film.

In both Kubrick's and Clarke's accounts, the meaning of the end of the Odyssey is pretty much an open question. Even at the point of filming the scene in Boreham Wood, they had no idea what would happen to Bowman once they got him into that room. In early versions of the script, the astronaut just wandered around until he spied the monolith. However, at the last moment, it was decided that Bowman should be transformed into the superman–Star-Child–thing, described by Clarke as a parapsychic member of a cosmic intelligence, garbed as a fetus because it is his "mind's image of himself—soon to be disposed." Beyond this, the Star Child's future plans are left hanging. Clarke has him detonate the nuclear satellites orbiting Earth, a move Kubrick rejected for fear of giving the film the same ending as *Dr. Strangelove*. In the epilogue of *The Lost Worlds of*

2001, Clarke admits his uncertainty about the Star Child's intentions and the fate of mankind, a hedging on his part that goes back to the ending of "The Sentinel."

It is precisely this state of uncertainty and arousal that Kubrick intended to achieve in his "controlled dream," as he has called *2001.* Borrowing and adapting many of the ideas of Eisenstein and the early Soviet filmmakers, who believed that film had the power to condition audiences to accept an ideology, Kubrick, too, attempts a conditioning experiment, not very dissimilar from *A Clockwork Orange*'s Ludovico Treatment. The open ended plot is comparable to the eye clamps that force *A Clockwork*'s victim to keep watching the screen. The story of Moon-Watcher and Bowman keeps us from leaving the theatre, and because it is a difficult and ambiguous story, hopefully leaves us curious enough to head back to the theatre again, where the conditioning can be repeated and strengthened. The treatment itself consists of two stages. The first is a kind of relentless affectiveness or arousal, meant to work on us physically like the nausea-producing drug therapy in *A Clockwork.* This, Kubrick achieves with his nonstop flow of all the paraphernalia of technique— special effects, odd camera angles, odd colors, striking sets, an unorthodox sound track. Toward the end, the tension is unrelieved. Just when we think he has given us the ultimate cinematic mindbender of the future in the Star Gate sequence, he tops it surrealistically with the uncanny bed chamber—a prototype of *past world* history in alien territory. And this is topped by the final shot of the fetus—the last thing we expect Bowman to turn into, an image not associated with a superman but with mankind's own humble biology and placed out there among the stars.

The second stage is the one which should open the floodgates of unconscious association and mythology. It involves the playing with our expectations and the breakdown of our defenses with sudden reversals. In virtually every scene in *2001,* the extraordinary leads to and is counterbalanced by the perfectly ordinary, or vice versa. Dr. Floyd's remarkable space trip ends boxed-in in the strictly business-like conference room at Clavius. The almost ludicrously ordinary photographing of the visitors to the Tycho excavation is interrupted by the uncanny awakening of the monolith. Virtually every shot and scene is double-edged, hovering at the same time between past and future, organics and mechanics, magic and science. In much of the film, Kubrick reassures us with the unusual and shocks us with the usual. The Star Gate, for instance, is reassuring—it's what we expect from science fiction. But we don't expect the very worldly bed chamber that follows; it is inappropriate to science fiction. The combination of the two throws us off balance. Even the absence of specific gravity in space is used to break down fundamental conventions of up and down, right and left, center and periphery. A pen hangs in the middle of the screen, a stewardess walks up a wall and out a door at the top of the frame, astronauts eat upside-down, rooms form a continuous curve without floor or ceiling. People move with painstaking exaggeration; arms and legs seem to float away from their owners, out of control; a voice (HAL's) is detached from its speaker. Explosions occur in silence; waltzes are heard where no music should be. We see pink oceans with purple waves and landscapes of orange mountains and a star-sized fetus among the stars.

The association of relentless arousal and sudden reversal theoretically produces, not the robotized citizen of *A Clockwork Orange,* but a lowered consciousness and a heightened awareness in an audience that can supposedly be "turned on," despite itself, to the substructure of mythology and message in *2001.* The point of this conditioning is debatable. At the very least, going back to Kubrick's original query about the dual nature of man, it should increase understanding (intelligence) by way of controlled sensation (feeling). In the end, we should have some, perhaps intuitive, perhaps half-realized idea of what the film is "about."

Kubrick's conditioning of his audience is directly related to *2001's* grim vision of man as a conditioned, or programmed, species, totally without will. The film documents his descent into complete passivity (the fate of the conditioned audience.) The original violent instincts of Moon-Watcher are satiated by his tools. Later, he eats to keep from starving, not to enjoy the kill. In the year *2001,* man has no hungers at all, or rather, his hungers have been transferred to the machines that do all the work and feel all the feelings. Man is still eating just to keep from starving. Aboard Discovery, he eats an unappetizing kind of paste, although pictures on his tray tell him what he is supposed to be tasting. The dozing, the hibernating, the boredom, the deadly "technish" that robs language of its breadth, the lack of emotions, the isolation of people (Dr. Floyd alone in Orion, Bowman in his pod), are all the effects of determinism. Even when Bowman is locked out of Discovery, he doesn't break in, he is *thrust* in by explosives, once more the passive instrument of his own tool. In the final sequence in the room, he is only momentarily conscious of the alterations of his own body, alterations he regards inertly, without terror or rage. The formal last supper appears from nowhere. Bowman has become an invalid in spirit, unable in the end to get his own food. He eats without consciousness, unlike Dr. Floyd who at least shows alertness about food, or the apes who eat raw meat with gusto. When Bowman accidently breaks his glass, his last tool is gone along with his last source of instinctual outlet. He becomes as defenseless as the Pleistocene apes, but without their primal frustrations. It is as if his transformation has bled him dry. He is man without instincts, already psychologically like the fetus he turns into. Presumably, super-man will be in complete control of himself, not having to contend with the disrupting influence of feelings. He will be passive because he will have no wish to be active, having no frustrations to work against.

While feelings and will are increasingly constricted in *2001*, intelligence is increasingly expansive, moving from "in" to "out" on a universal scale. Using the four monoliths to indicate a spatial and intellectual leap in the history of mankind at four given moments of time, Kubrick shows the ape-man extending himself from cave to world; turn of the century man, from world to moon; twenty-first century man, from moon to solar system; super-man, from solar system to universe. Tools go through a similar progression from the bone thrown a short distance into Earth air, to the space craft that break out of Earth gravity, to HAL who drives Discovery beyond Jupiter, to the completely unrestricted monoliths in space. Clarke takes the matter further, in his novel, where the aliens are also breaking out—of their own flesh. When Moon-Watcher slays the tapir, the aliens are described in the book as living spaceships. But by the time Bowman hits the Star Gate, they are jumping freely from star to star, having rid themselves of all material existence. By inference, they are being programmed by something even higher up the chain, perhaps the cosmic mind Clarke alludes to. As the uterine imagery of the film suggests, the whole universe is in a state of growth. It too is breaking out of the macrocosm into the unimaginable supermacrocosm. Mankind, tools, and aliens are all caught up in a law of universal expansion—at the price of freedom of choice.

Kubrick emphasizes the edgy balance between the confinement of will and the breaking out of consciousness in imagery that is claustrophobic and agoraphobic at the same time. The Cinerama screen lends itself to an agoraphobic kind of spaciousness. But within the frame, man is restricted to the small confines of his "life support systems." From the apes huddled in their small cave in the middle of a mammoth desert to Bowman trapped in his pod in the middle of the vast Star Gate, we see mankind swaddled in space suits and space craft (his technology) and finally his own aging body, protective barriers against the unknown rigours of both physical and mental space.

In the context of Kubrick's determinism, the monolith as a symbol, and the mythology associated with it, can be interpreted on (again) four levels:

(1) As a symbol of alien technology, technology in general, and the "robotized" aspects of human nature—the cold, featureless and impregnable logic of the universe and the mind. Parallels with the myth of Frankenstein, slight in the film but pointed in the novel, suggest that technology (and, by extension, intelligence) is the monstrous creation of passionate man, bound to turn against him as does HAL aboard Discovery.

(2) A symbol of predestined fate, whether we call it an alien life-form, a cosmic mind, or God—abstract and evil (black) in the sense that it turns life into a passive clockwork, without the power of self-determination or choice. The corrupted biblical imagery, from "The Dawn of Man's" corrupted Genesis to Tycho's black mass to the last episode's corrupted Passion, suggest the satanic malevolence of the cosmic design, at least as man perceives it.

(3) As previously mentioned, a Jungian symbol of consciousness (intelligence)—the only saving grace life has in a strictly deterministic universe. Parallels with the *Odyssey* belong in this category. HAL is the one-eyed cyclops the film's Ulysses must fight on the round-about voyage that brings him back home as a Star Child and King—a being of greater consciousness and self-control, thus a fit ruler.

(4) As a box, a Freudian symbol of the womb, bringing together all the erotic and fetal imagery of the film.

This last interpretation deserves elaboration. *2001* is a science-fiction film without visible outer-space monsters and without the seemingly superfluous love interest that usually give the game away for Freudian critics. The sensual elements in the film occur entirely in the abstract couplings of spacecraft, blunted even further by the strictly clinical associations of uterine life. Everything conspires in *2001* to rob the situation of all passion. Typically for a Kubrick film, women are absent—unless we count the nominal appearances of the antiseptic stewardess in white or the sedate Russian ladies in black. Dr. Floyd, who sleeps through a love scene televised on Orion, is clearly unmoved by his fleeting moments with the women, who have completely disappeared by the time the action gets down to the serious business at Tycho. Discovery, of course, has no women members of its crew, a situation Clarke says the men deal with pharmaceutically. This lack of love interest in the plot is related to the film's progressive breakdown of family life. In the first episode, baby chimps are present in what seems to be a family-type gathering (although, significantly, Kubrick refers to the apes as "the boys"). Dr. Floyd phones his home on Earth to discover that his wife is "out" and Rachael, the caretaker of his daughter, is inaccessible. He tells Squirt he won't be coming to her birthday party—a family reunion is impossible. A short time later, the Russian lady, Elena, matter-of-factly admits that her husband is at the bottom of the sea on Earth, a *de facto* separation from his wife in space. Eighteen months later, no one in the film is married. Poole cannot answer or respond to a birthday greeting from his parents, who discuss insurance policies instead of family intimacies. Clarke takes pains to describe the astronaut's meagre Earth ties to family and girl friends. They are chosen for the mission, in part, because of their ability to cope without women during the long voyage. Bowman has no Penelope to flee from or return to; he escapes instead from the women and family ties represented by "mother" Earth in the abstract. The theme of sexual self-sufficiency—as old a theme in Western literature as Homer and Plato—is projected once again.

The Star Child returns to his homeworld with uncertain intentions, planning, perhaps, to destroy the imperfect biology of a species consisting in part of women, a sex the whole film denies and negates. In a Freudian sense, *2001* concerns a regression to an idea of earliest childhood, when the infant is happily unaware of any difference between the sexes, believing that men somehow produce the babies. The film, very typically for Kubrick, is a disguised quest for this kind of masculine self-sufficiency which includes childbirth without women. Kubrick uses imagery to try out machine birth among the space craft and stellar birth in the Star Gate, while the plot leads up to the ultimate in masculine childbirth fantasies, when Bowman bypasses all biological difficulties by turning into a fetal infant himself. Bowman is the father and the son, and he did it without a woman—*that* is the final triumph of the film that, on other levels, suggests that the individual is a completely passive being.

From this perspective, the plot of *2001* can be retold as an expression of an infantile daydream. The monolith—a fearsome power in a box (the womb)—can be taken as a representation of an alien or external traumatic event that once caused the individual to become aware of sexual differentiation. This occurred during early childhood, four million years ago in psychological time (perhaps around the age of four). Instantly, the world was divided between those who have tools (male genitalia—a comparison first made explicit in *Dr. Strangelove*) and those who don't, forcing the individual on to the very mixed blessings of adulthood in the twentieth century. But at some hoped-for moment in the near future (2001), the individual discovers a way to regain the pleasurable sense of oneness that preceded that traumatic event in the past. Memory of the original trauma is dug up (the moon monolith), and this experience somehow permits the individual to destroy the tool (HAL) that has become so demanding and so problematic. Afterward, he can restore the delicious state of helplessness and passivity he knew as a baby, without, however, the infant's corresponding pain of hunger. In the guise of aging, in which sexual powers are lost, he can regress further and further back in time until a final confrontation with his trauma (the last monolith) transforms the individual into a unity of father–mother–baby—the superman-Star Child, giving birth to himself and controlling the universe without the need of tools or a specified sexuality.

Many of the mythic and literary references in the film add strength to this fantasy. The Eveless Genesis in which women are *not* cursed with childbearing; the mission to Jupiter, the planet named for the god who bore a child (Athena) through his head; the comparison between the HAL episode and the story of Frankenstein, in which a man also single-handedly creates his own child-monster; and the corrupted Passion of the last episode, in which crucifixion, resurrection, and virgin birth are simultaneously experienced by a single man.

One of the remaining questions about *2001* is whether Kubrick's conditioning experiment is ultimately used to reveal or conceal this fantasy. Does evolution represent the wish to evolve out of the individual's adult, sexualized state? Does predestination represent the desire to escape blame for the wish that cannot be abolished? Is intelligence a substitute for the infant's dream of self-sufficiency? Is the interest in victimization by extraterrestrials a cover-up for a desire for passivity? In the film, the conceptual themes (levels 1–3) and the most deeply mythic theme (level 4) remain in conflict. Such conflict is typical of science fiction, which often uses social and moral concerns as a screen for repressed sexual desires. (See Margaret Tarrat's "Monsters From the Id," *Films and Filming,* December 1970.)

In *The Making of 2001,* Kubrick admits that *2001* "attempts to communicate more to the subconscious and to the feelings than it does to the intellect." Similarly, in a *Playboy* interview (September 1968), he says, "I intended the film to be an intensely subjective experience that reaches the viewer at an inner level of consciousness." If so, perhaps the penultimate query about the film should look ahead to Kubrick's next work, *A Clockwork Orange,* which develops the idea of film as a conditioning mechanism. Whole schools of psychologists have questioned the effect of film upon the audience, although the answer is not yet in. Perhaps we should at least roughly touch upon the ethics of a filmmaker like Kubrick, who deliberately uses the frosty logic of film technique to manipulate and control us, his audience, at our deepest and most vulnerable fiber of being. While we are being seduced by a cleverly camouflaged fantasy or by philosophical content or even by a breathtaking vision of the future, we should wonder if we are being subtly altered by what appears, despotically, on the screen.

summary critique

2001 may be the only film made thus far to be supplied with its own footnotes in the form of four books published after the film's release. Arthur C. Clarke's novel, *2001: A Space Odyssey*, is a version of the prose screenplay of *2001* that was published in July 1968, three months after the film's preview in New York. Jerome Agel, who is better known for his published collaborations with Marshall McLuhan, edited *The Making of Kubrick's 2001*, an interesting collage of documents, photographs, letters, and other material related to the film, published in April 1970. The anthology introduces its readers to the kind of McLuhanesque nonlinear thinking Kubrick intended to convey in *2001*. It includes Clarke's short story, "The Sentinel"; a transcript of the ten-minute prologue originally intended to open the film; ninety-six pages of stills from the film with commentary by Kubrick, Clarke, Trumbull, and Pederson; a good selection of reviews of the film as well as profiles of and interviews with Kubrick; and a cartoon parody of *2001* first printed in *Mad Magazine*. Alexander Walker's *Stanley Kubrick Directs* (1971) is a critical study of Kubrick's work based on extensive interviews with the director and written with the shadow of Kubrick across every page. Clarke's *The Lost Worlds of 2001* (1972) contains extracts from both the screenwriter's log (for which the calendar in this guide is partially indebted) and the first version of the prose screenplay as well as three alternate endings for *2001*. Hints from Clarke's log suggest that Kubrick may have actually masterminded the publication of these four books, perhaps to help an audience not expected to "get" the film on its own. In his most recent book of scientific speculations, *Report on Planet Three* (1972), Clarke returns once more to the film that may still baffle his fans, reprinting two articles about *2001:* one written during the production of the film, "Son of Dr. Strangelove, Or, How I Learned to Stop Worrying and Love Stanley Kubrick," and another, "The Myth of *2001,*" which Clarke claims "is the only one I have written (or intend to write) *after* the release of the film" (p. 246). Essentially, both articles are clipped paraphrases of material appearing in *The Lost Worlds of 2001.*

Although security was tight in the studio during the filming of *2001,* Kubrick had been leaking information about the film for more than two years before its release. As early as January 16, 1966, Hollis Alpert wrote a long biographical sketch of Kubrick for *The New York Sunday Times Magazine,* called "Offbeat Director in Outer Space," which included enticing references to the director's then current consultations with industrial and scientific corporations. In the following spring, *Sight and Sound* published Dave Robinson's "Two for the Sci-fi," which refused to disclose the "secret" plot of *2001* but did reveal that "N.A.S.A. put its computers at [Kubrick's] disposal to work out the actual trajectory to Jupiter." By the time the film appeared, expectations were high; the public had been prepared for a very unorthodox and ambitious film. Some professional critics, however, greeted the film with a jaundiced eye, made even more skeptical by all the "hype" of the film's advance publicity.

Vincent Canby, after seeing *2001* a second time, summed up the critical response to the film as of May 3, 1970, as follows: "The film opened to almost unanimous pans from the daily press and then went on to become a cult film, a head film, a film to recant by, and a smashing commercial success" (*The New York Sunday Times,* Section 2, p. 1). Apologists for the initial pans, however, point out that most of the New York reviewers attended the press previews on April 1 and 2, 1968, two days *before* Kubrick cut an additional nineteen minutes of the slowest-moving footage from the film. Thus, nearly all of the first reviewers complained of boredom. In the first *New York Times* review, for instance, Renata Adler found *2001* "somewhere between hypnotic and hopelessly boring" (April 4, 1968, p. 58). *Newsweek's* Joseph Morgenstern called parts of it "a crashing bore," claiming that Kubrick's "potentially majestic myth . . . dwindles into a whimsical space operetta, then frantically inflates itself again for a surreal climax in which the imagery is just obscure enough to be annoying, just precise enough to be banal" (April 15, 1968, p. 97). *New York's* Judith Crist, titling her review "Stanley Kubrick, Please Come Down," charged the film with "an attenuated and frequently tedious narrative that provides watered-down adventure and a dash of metaphysical theorizing that might kindly be called 'enigmatic' " (April 22, 1968, p. 52). Recalling his first impression of *2001*, Stanley Kauffmann found the film "so dull, it even dulls our interest in the technical ingenuity for the sake of which Kubrick has allowed it to become dull" (*Figures of Light*, p. 72), and even upon a second viewing, he "thought that the cuts did little to help the sagging, although the fact that they had been made at all contravene those admirers of the picture who say that Kubrick was not concerned with such matters as action and suspense" (p. 74).

Perhaps the most scathing attacks appear in Pauline Kael's "Trash, Art, and the Movies," originally written for *Harper's Magazine* and reprinted in *Going Steady,* and in an anonymous item called "2001: The First Space Ship Introduced Out of a High Flying Thighbone" in *The New York Free Press* (April 11, 1968). The latter discusses HAL's latent homosexuality, the film's visual content that is "like a six-month trial subscription to *Life* magazine," and its resulting "giganticism enveloping a rather clever but definitely minor anecdote" (p. 9–10). Kael, who sees *2001* as "a kind of sci-fi nut's fantasy" (p. 121), says,

"*2001* may be no more than trash in the latest, up-to-the-minute guises, using 'artistic techniques' to give trash the look of art. The serious art look may be the latest fashion in *expensive* trash" (p. 117). She concludes, "if big film directors are to get credit for doing badly what others have been doing brilliantly for years with no money, just because they've put it on a big screen, then businessmen are greater than poets and theft is art" (p. 124).

Andrew Sarris, the influential auteurist critic for *The Village Voice,* was apparently so offended by Kubrick's unsportsman-like cuts made *after* the press previews, that he refused to comment upon *2001* until February 20, 1969. He then damned the film with faint praise, conceding that "a case can be made for '2001: A Space Odyssey' on the basis of its presumably mean-ingful boredom and its adolescent sci-fi pessimism" (p. 47). As an auteurist, Sarris dislikes conceptual cinema for theoretical reasons, a dislike that he seems to have had confirmed once more with *2001.* Thus, in his directors' pantheon published in *The American Cinema* (1968), Sarris places Kubrick in the category of "Strained Seriousness," reserved for "talented but uneven directors with the mortal sin of pretentiousness" (p. 189). Meanwhile, in a move to counter the effects of Sarris' con-spiracy of silence in *The Village Voice,* on May 2, 1968, M.G.M. bought a full page in the paper facing Sarris' regular column and there reprinted what must be *2001*'s most ecstatic review: Gene Youngblood's "Stanley Kubrick's '2001': A Masterpiece" from *The Los Angeles Free Press* (April 19, 1968), which discov-ered in "a million dollar corporate investment" and "a personal artistic statement" a combination "every underground movie-maker dreams of." Devoting two chapters to the film in his book, *Expanded Cinema* (1970), Youngblood calls the film an "epochal achievement of cinema" (p. 139) and "a technical masterpiece" (p. 140).

Even in the criticism favorable to *2001,* there is confusion about the film's meaning. Typically, *The New Yorker's* Penelope Gilliatt trusts to her senses and calls it "some sort of great film, and an unforgettable endeavor" (April 13, 1968, p. 150). Similarly, in London's *The Observer Review,* Tom Milne says "it is worth watching anyway no matter what it *means*" (May 5, 1968, p. 29) and in *Sight and Sound,* Mel McKee frankly writes that *2001* is about "something," adding, "and that something is more a philosophical abstraction than a mere step forward in plot" (Autumn 1969, p. 206).

Currently, *2001's* reputation rests, in part, on its technical achievements. The special effects work in the film is often original, often novel, certainly an extension of basic cinema vocabulary. Significantly, the technically-oriented *American Cinematographer* is the only film journal to have devoted a whole issue to *2001*—June 1968—including an article by the film's special effects supervisor, Douglas Trumbull. As Tim Hunter (et al.) reminds us, however, *2001* "cannot be easily judged if only because of its dazzling technical perfection. To be able to see beyond that may take a few years. When we have grown used to . . . the wonder of Kubrick's special effects . . . , then we can probe confidently beyond *2001's* initial fascination and decide what kind of a film it really is" ("2001: A Space Odyssey," *Film Heritage* with the permission of *The Harvard Crimson,* Summer 1968, p. 20).

Perhaps the acid test of *2001's* impact on film criticism can be found in the pages of almost any general study of film published since 1968, where the debate about the film's strengths and weaknesses rages on. And where words fail, we can find the influence of *2001* extending beyond criticism to conscious imitation and parody—in, for instance, advertisements and children's television. The film has already left its mark on wider circles than the film industry—it has become a part of our culture.

a Kubrick filmography
bibliography
rental sources

a Kubrick filmography

Day of the Flight (1951)
Flying Padre (1951)
Fear and Desire (1953)
Killer's Kiss (1955)
The Killing (1956)
Paths of Glory (1957)
Spartacus (1959–60)
Lolita (1961)
Dr. Strangelove, or How I Learned to Stop Worrying and Love the Bomb (1963)
2001: A Space Odyssey (1968)
A Clockwork Orange (1971)

bibliography

All items marked with an asterisk (*) are anthologized, usually in excerpted form, in Jerome Agel's *The Making of Kubrick's 2001.*

*Adler, Renata. "The Screen: '2001' is Up, Up, and Away." *New York Times,* 4 April 1968, 58.

Adler, Renata. "Astronauts, Maoists—and Girls." *New York Times,* 21 April 1968, Sec. 4, 1D, and 28D. A second, unfavorable look at *2001,* reviewed with Godard's *La Chinoise* and Jacque Demy's *The Young Girls of Rochefort.*

Agel, Jerome, ed. *The Making of Kubrick's 2001.* New York: New American Library, 1970.

Alpert, Hollis. "Offbeat Director in Outer Space." *The New York Sunday Times Magazine,* 16 January 1966, 14–15, 40–41, 43, 46, 51.

Alpert, Hollis. "2001: A Space Odyssey." *Film 68/69.* Eds.

Hollis Alpert and Andrew Sarris. New York: Simon & Schuster, 1969, 57–60. Generally favorable reactions to accuracy of effects, music and imagery of film, although "somehow we expected more than we get."

Austen, David. "2001: A Space Odyssey." *Films and Filming,* 14 (July 1968), 24–27. "*2001* is concerned with faith, that is, belief without rational proof, and as such it must be a personal experience for each individual spectator" (p. 24).

*Bernstein, Jeremy. "Profiles: How About a Little Game?" *The New Yorker,* 12 November 1966, 70–72, passim. A biographical sketch of Kubrick and an introduction to his films and methods of filmmaking. A note on Arthur Clarke, his collaboration with Kubrick on *2001,* and a synopsis of "The Sentinel." The author describes his visit to the Boreham Wood studios in the summer of 1965.

Canby, Vincent. "Spaced Out by Stanley." *New York Times,* 3 May 1970, Sec. 2, 1 and 21.

*Crist, Judith. "Stanley Kubrick, Please Come Down." *New York,* 22 April 1968, 52–53.

Ciment, Michel. "L'Odyssée de Stanley Kubrick: Part III: Vers l'Infini—*2001.*" *Positif,* No. 98 (October 1968), 14–20. Scientific philosophy and existential content of film analysed with references to Aurel David, Pascal, Norbert Wiener, Werner Heisenberg.

*Clarke, Arthur C. "The Sentinel." In *Expedition to Earth,* 1954; rpt. London: Sphere Books Limited, 1968, 163–74.

———. *2001: A Space Odyssey.* New York: New American Library, 1968.

———. *The Lost Worlds of 2001.* New York: New American Library, 1972.

———. *Report on Planet Three: And Other Speculations.* New York: Harper & Row, 1972.

Cluny, Michel Claude. *2001: l'Odysée de l'Espace.* Dossiers du

Cinéma, Films 1, eds. Jean-Louis Bory and Claude Michel Cluny, Paris: Casterman, 1971. A four-page pamphlet including M. Cluny's highly laudatory article, quotes from Kubrick and critics, a biographical note, synopsis, and credits.

Daniels, Don. "2001: A New Myth." *Film Heritage*, 3 (Summer 1968), 1–9. General discussion of themes and techniques in *2001*.

*Del Rey, Lester. "2001: A Space Odyssey." *Galaxy Magazine*, 26 (July 1968), 193–94. Unfavorable review by a science-fiction critic who complains that "this isn't a normal science-fiction movie at all."

Dempewolff, Richard. "How They Made 2001." *Science Digest*, 63 (May 1968), 34–39. Light, technical account of production written after a visit to the Boreham Wood studios. Describes stewardess' "up-side-down" walk, centrifuge, weightless effects.

Dumont, Jean Paul and Jean Monod. *Le Foetus Astral*. Paris: Editions Christian Bourgeois, 1970. Perhaps the first full-length structuralist study of a film. *2001* is explicated using the methodology of the structural study of myth worked out by Claude Lévi-Strauss and the structural study of linguistics worked out by Ferdinand de Sassure. The authors find that the film is constructed of an "immense variation on a few elementary forms in three colors" (p. 15). Using graphs, they chart the transformations of such basic forms as the sun, moon, bone, and monolith.

Eisenschitz, Bernard. "La Marge." *Cahiers du Cinéma*, No. 209 (February 1969), 56–57. Lauditory review of "un film sans message" by an independent American filmmaker in exile.

"Fanciful Leap Across the Ages." *Life*, 64 (5 April 1968), 24–35. Fourteen color stills from *2001* and, on pages 34–35, a review by Albert Rosenfeld, who compares the film with *Moby Dick*.

Geduld, Harry M. "Return to Méliès: Reflections on the Science-Fiction Film." *The Humanist,* 28 (November/December 1968), 23–24, 28. Reviews *2001* as an anti-humanist film in the tradition of the primitivist science-fiction filmmaker Méliès, who also seemed to indicate that man is the mere pawn of cosmic forces.

Gelmis, Joseph. "Stanley Kubrick." In *The Film Director as Superstar*. Garden City, New York: Doubleday & Company, 1970, 293–316.

*Gilliatt, Penelope. "After Man." *The New Yorker,* 13 April 1968, 150–52.

*Hunter, Tim, et al., comps. "2001: A Space Odyssey." *Film Heritage,* 3 (Summer 1968), 12–20. First published in *The Harvard Crimson*.

Kagan, Norman. *The Cinema of Stanley Kubrick*. New York: Holt, Rinehart and Winston, 1972. Useful compendium of director's work and methodology.

*Kael, Pauline. "Trash, Art, and the Movies." In *Going Steady*. Boston: Little, Brown & Co., 1970. First published in *Harper's* magazine.

*Kauffmann, Stanley. "2001." In *Figures of Light*. New York: Harper & Row, 1971, 70–75. First published in *The New Republic*.

Kinder, Marsha and Beverle Houston. "2001: A Space Odyssey." In *Close-Up: A Critical Perspective on Film*. New York: Harcourt Brace Jovanovich, 1972, 85–92. Off-beat comparison of technology in *2001* and the history of film technique: still photography and silent cinema in "The Dawn of Man," the talkies in the second and third episodes, underground film in the Star Gate sequence.

Kloman, William. "In 2001, Will Love Be a Seven-Letter Word?" *New York Times,* 14 April 1968, Sec. 2, 5D. An interview with Kubrick touching on the basic metaphysical and scientific themes in *2001*.

Kohler, Charlie. "Stanley Kubrick Raps." *Eye,* August 1968, 84–86. Kubrick answers questions about scientific accuracy in *2001,* costumes, his collaboration with Clarke, the centrifuge, the ending, his earlier films, and how to learn filmmaking.

Kozloff, Max. "2001." *Film Culture,* No. 48–49 (Winter and Spring 1970), 53–56. One of the most thoughtful articles on *2001.* General discussion of scientific and metaphysical themes as well as interesting aesthetic arguments about scale and movement in the film.

Lightman, Herb A. "Filming *2001: A Space Odyssey.*" *American Cinematographer,* 49 (June 1968), 412–14, passim. Written after a visit to the Boreham Wood studios in the fall of 1967, this article introduces the issue of *American Cinematographer* devoted to *2001.* Included are a plot synopsis, biographical note, and technical discussion of special effects, shots of weightlessness, shooting in the centrifuge.

————. "Front Projection for *2001: A Space Odyssey.*" *American Cinematographer,* 49 (June 1968), 420–22, passim. A highly technical description of the front-projection for background transparencies in "The Dawn of Man."

McKee, Mel. "2001: Out of the Silent Planet." *Sight and Sound,* 38 (Autumn 1969), 204–07.

Michelson, Annette, "Bodies in Space: Film as 'Carnal Knowledge.' " *Artforum,* 7 (February 1969), 54–63. Abstract and obscure analysis of *2001* with references to Debussy, Dégas, Robbe-Grillet, Stravinsky, Chekov, Wagner, Plato.

Milne, Tom. "A Visionary En Voyage." *The Observer Review,* 5 May 1968, 29.

*Morgenstern, Joseph. "Kubrick's Cosmos." *Newsweek,* 15 April 1968, 97 and 100.

*Norden, Eric. "Playboy Interview: Stanley Kubrick." *Playboy,* 15 (September 1968), 85–86, passim. The longest interview Kubrick has granted, covering his prognostications about the future and allusions to *2001*'s "visual" message. A plot synopsis and critical summary of the film and a biographical sketch are included.

Phillips, Gene. "Kubrick." *Film Comment,* 7 (Winter 1971–72), 30–34. An interview covering Kubrick's whole career, with pages 33–34 on the basic scientific implications of *2001*.

Pohl, Frederik. "2001: A Second Look." *Film Society Review,* 5 (February 1970), 23–27. The editor of *Galaxy* feels the film "represents wasted opportunity. For all that talent and and all that money it could have been *good* science fiction."

Rapf, Maurice. "A Talk with Stanley Kubrick." *Action,* 4 (January–February 1969), 15–18. Kubrick discusses his collaboration with Clarke, his admiration for Chaplin and Welles, the reviews of *2001*.

Robinson, Dave. "Two for the Sci-fi." *Sight and Sound,* 35 (Spring 1966), 57–61.

Romi, Yvette. "Deux Hommes et Deux Femmes: 4) Kubrick: 2001." *midi/minuit Fantastique,* No. 22 (Summer 1970), 72–73. An interview with Clarke, discussing 2001's Freudian, Nietzschian, and religious messages.

Sarris, Andrew. "Stanley Kubrick." In *The American Cinema.* New York: Dutton, 1968, 195–96.

————. "Films." *The Village Voice,* 20 February 1969, 47.

Shatnoff, Judith. "A Gorilla to Remember." *Film Quarterly,* 22 (Fall 1968), 56–62. A mixed review of *2001* with a less enthusiastic review of *Planet of the Apes.* Favors *2001*'s "celebration of technology," birth imagery, and visual effects, while objecting to its "creaky old plot."

Stine, Harry G. "2001: A Space Odyssey." *Analog Science Fiction/Science Fact,* 82 (November 1968), 167–68. " 'Star Trek' is doing a better job with a lot less money and fanfare."

Stover, Leon E. "Apeman, Superman—Or 2001's Answer to the World's Riddle." *Amazing Stories,* March 1969, 137–41.

Discussion of the film's implications of good and evil in a universe "made full with the essential goodness of a disembodied humanity."

Trumbull, Douglas. "Creating Special Effects for 2001." *American Cinematographer,* 49 (June 1968), 416–19, passim. The best description of how it was done by the film's special effects supervisor. Technical information about keeping accurate records of "held-takes," animated effects, matting techniques, lighting problems, model construction, the Slit-Scan machine, front projection, shooting in the centrifuge.

"2001: The First Space Ship Introduced Out of a High Flying Thighbone." *The New York Free Press,* 11 April 1968, 9–10.

Walker, Alexander. *Stanley Kubrick Directs.* New York: Harcourt Brace Jovanovich, 1971.

Youngblood, Gene. "Stanley Kubrick's '2001': A Masterpiece." *The Los Angeles Free Press,* 19 April 1968. Rpt. in *The Village Voice,* 2 May 1968, 44.

————. "The New Nostalgia." In *Expanded Cinema,* New York: E. P. Dutton, 1970, 139–56. "New nostalgia" is defined as "an awareness of radical evolution in the living present." Application to *2001* and discussion of its philosophical content, death and birth imagery, confusion of ideas, and its "minimalist aesthetic of primary structures."

rental source

A 16mm sound-color-anamorphic print of the film can be rented from Films Incorporated, 4420 Oakton Street, Skokie, Illinois 60076.